The Composite Plates of Audubon's

Birds of America

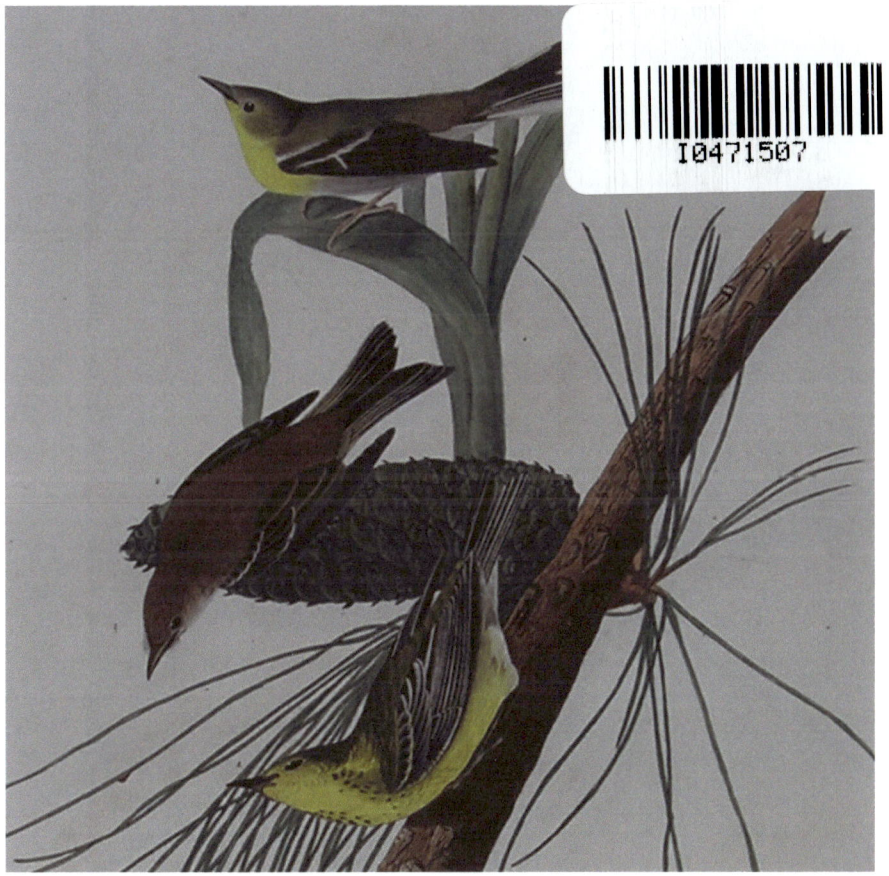

Jeff Holt and Albert Filemyr

ISBN: 1-4392-1318-6

ISBN-13: 978-1439213186

Library of Congress Control Number: 2008908973

Cover Image: Detail from the Maryland Yellow Throat or Yellow-breasted Warbler Composite Plate

Title Page: Detail from the Pine Creeping Warbler Composite Plate

Table of Contents

Illustration Credits

The Composite Plates of Audubon's *Birds of America*

Jeff Holt and Albert Filemyr

[Authors Note: The terms "plate" and "print" are used interchangeably throughout this publication. These terms are used to refer to the finished hand colored images that were printed on double elephant folio size paper. "Plate" and "print" should not be confused with the metal "copper plates" from which a finished "plate" or" print" is produced.]

Background

While John James Audubon is justifiably revered as an artist and ornithologist, his work was not without faults. For instance, to this day, the identities of five birds depicted by Audubon in his *Birds of America* remain a puzzle to the ornithological community.[1] Such errors, however, must be considered within the context of the time. Early chroniclers of North America's avifauna were in many cases, making identification of collected specimens with little or no reliable reference material with which to consult. As Audubon's predecessor, Alexander Wil-

---

[1] One such example is the Small-Headed Flycatcher, which became a central figure in Audubon's infamous dispute with members of the Philadelphia scientific community. For a more thorough discussion on Audubon's mystery birds, see *Notes on Audubon's "Mystery" Birds*, Cassinia, Vol. 70: 22-24.

son observed, "Such is the barrenness of the best European works on the feathered tribes of the United States, and so numerous are the mistakes (to call them by the gentlest name) with which they are disfigured, that little has been, or indeed can be, derived from that quarter." (Wilson, 1808-14, Vol. 3) Thus, Audubon, Wilson and their contemporaries were forced by necessity to make identifications using little more than the knowledge they gained through studious observation and specimen collecting using their trusted shooting pieces. In the case of Audubon's *The Birds of America*, considering the magnitude of the work (435 plates depicting 508 species and 1065 individual birds), it is a marvel that so few errors appear. To Audubon's credit, during the lengthy period of time it took to bring the entire work to completion (1826 to 1838), Audubon recognized that his knowledge had increased and that errors existed in the finished product, which he publicly acknowledged.[2] To correct some of these deficiencies, before the copper plates were shipped to America, Audubon instructed his engraver, Robert Havell, Jr.[3] to create what are now commonly known as "composite plates". Simply, Havell was asked to take the bird depicted on one plate and add it to those already depicted on a separate plate, thus creating a unique print that combined two previously published plates into one.[4]

This publication endeavors to explore the background and unique characteristics associated with the "composite plates".

---

[2] In a letter dated September 15, 1835 to his friend, Rev. John Bachman, Audubon writes: " My principal Wish in the finishing of my Letter press, i.e. the fourth Volume of it, is to bring in it a good and close comparative anatomical account of the Type of each of our Ornithological species by which I now think, the least errors committed by my predecessors or by Myself heretofore can at once be detected and *corrected!!*" (Corning, Vol. 2, 1930)

[3] Early in the publishing of *Birds of America*, two other individuals were involved in the engraving and production process, William Lizars and Robert Havell, Sr. These individuals' involvement in the project had long since terminated by the time the decision was made to produce the composite plates.

[4] As an example, Selby's Flycatcher appeared as plate IX in Volume 1 of *The Birds of America*. In creating a composite plate, Havell printed the Selby's Flycatcher image onto plate CX, which already contained a depiction of the male and female Hooded Warbler.

In a series of three letters written from Edinburgh to Havell in London, we find the following instructions regarding the authorization to produce the composite plates:

The first letter is dated August 20, 1838 and is written by Audubon's son, Victor Gifford Audubon to Havell and to which, John James appended the following: "You recollect I dare say that you promised to print for me 6 copies of the plates that have the old bird on one and the young or the female on some other. I have promised one to B. Phillips, another to Ed. Harris, and want 4 (next two words indecipherable). Should you be puzzled in making out the species after looking over the whole work, write to me, and I will send you a list of them, but I think you will have no difficulty after looking for them yourself." (J.J. Audubon, 1838, *in litt.*)

Eight days later (August 28, 1838) Victor writes to Havell; "I will send the list of plates &c. to print the setts as soon as I can, meantime, each plate had the name of every bird on it, so that you can look out some of them if you wish at once...My father only wants the 6 copies printed of these plates which have old or young birds to add onto them or females &c." (V.G. Audubon, 1838, *in litt.*)

Finally, on September 26, 1838, Victor again sends a third communiqué to Havell which includes the following: "I send you herewith the lists of birds to be placed on the different plates, and we want you to use your own good taste in placing them to the best effect...The additional prints you will please print so to make all 6 setts of these particular plates extra, if you find they look well.... They are to be extra plates only, so that you needn't use any but the coppers on which they are (indecipherable). We will keep them for ourselves, Mr. Phillips & Mr. Harris." (V.G. Audubon, 1838, *in litt.*)

Unfortunately for posterity, the "list" referred to in the last letter has not been located by the authors. Hence, we do not know who wrote the "list" (John James or Victor) and whether or not Havell was faithful to the "list" in producing the composite plates. As will be shown, the absence of the "list" is critical link in potentially explaining many of the unanswered questions regarding these unique plates.

One researcher has noted that while "legend has it that 6 prints were pulled from each of the 13 plates but 7 prints have been found for one of the plates, so perhaps there are more than 6 prints of the other plates." (Fries, 1973) Given the succinct nature of these instructions, one is left to ponder why Havell produced more than that which had been ordered. Furthermore, why did Audubon request the production of more than three sets at all? Of the 6 (or 7) sets of composite prints produced, as the above letters indicate, 3 sets were destined to be bound into Audubon's personal copy and those of his close friends, Dr. Benjamin Phillips and Edward Harris. The Audubon and Phillips copies with all 13 composite prints have survived and are presently housed at the Stark Museum of Art in Orange, Texas and the Field Museum of Natural History in Chicago respectively. The whereabouts of the Harris set is unknown. "Incomplete evidence suggests it was broken up." (Low, 2002)[5] The remaining unbound prints became part of the excess stock that Audubon brought back from England, and, over the years, a number of these prints have been found in other complete sets of *Birds of America.*[6]

---

[5] The Audubon, Phillips and Harris sets were also bound not in the order in which the plates were produced but rather in the accepted taxonomic order of the day. See Appendix I.

[6] According to Fries's research, the following institutions were found to have in their possession composite prints:
    John James Audubon Center at Mill Grove – 8 prints
    Library of Parliament, Canada – 7 prints
    Bowdoin College – 4 prints

In analyzing the composite plates and the errors these were designed to correct, the 13 plates can be split into two groups. The first (and smaller) group involves the misidentification of a known species. In each of these prints, the misidentified species was believed by Audubon to be a newly discovered species and was accordingly given a name now relegated to ornithological history. The later group of composite prints involved the combining onto a single page (with one notable exception), previously properly identified species but of different sexes, ages or plumages.

Lehigh University – 2 prints
Yale University – 1 print
In addition to the above, a set formerly owned by the New York Society Library and broken up in 1980 contained 3 prints.

Misidentified Plates

Of the first category of composite prints involving incorrectly identified species, it is perhaps interesting to note that each of the three misidentified species described below were all part of the first volume of *Birds of America* and Audubon's written description of each also appears in the first volume (published in 1831) of *Ornithological Biography*, the companion text to *Birds of America.* Evidently, Audubon, like many who have followed, found it difficult to identify the "confusing fall warblers". The student of Audubon may find some of his comments regarding the "discovery" of these three species interesting.

Selby's Fly Catcher (plate IX) is an immature Hooded Warbler, and was therefore combined with the male and female of that species portrayed on plate CX. On Selby's Fly Catcher, which Audubon collected on July 1, 1821 in Louisiana; "As this bird, to the day on which my engraving of it appeared, had not been described, or, in as far as I know, obtained by any other person than myself, notwithstanding the great number of individuals who have of late years been searching our States for new and rare species, it must be considered as of very unfrequent occurrence, and probably as seldom going farther north or east than the place where I discovered it. Moreover, it is so scarce even there, that in all my walks I only shot three individuals, in the course of nine years." (Audubon, 1831-39, Vol. 1)

Roscoe's Yellow Throat (plate XXIV) is a hatch year male Common Yellowthroat and was combined with the mature male and female portrayed on plate XXIII, titled Maryland Yellow Throat. The Roscoe's Yellow Throat, specimen was collected by Audubon in a swamp in Mississippi in September, 1821. Interestingly, Audubon suspected that this bird was a Common Yellowthroat. "In general appearance, this species so much resembles the preceding, that had not its habits differed so greatly from those of the Maryland Yellow-throat, I might have been induced to consider it as merely an accidental variety. On examining it more closely, however, and on comparing it with that bird, I felt, as I now feel, fully confident of its being different." (Audubon, 1831-39, Vol. 1) Was Audubon fooled by the behavior of a bird seeking sustenance to fuel a lengthy migration?

Vigors Vireo or Vigor's Warbler (in plate XXX) is in fact an immature Pine Warbler and was added to the pair depicted on plate CXL (which bears the name Pine Creeping Warbler). The Vigor's Warbler was shot by Audubon in May of 1812 near Mill Grove, Pennsylvania. He states to "have never met with another of its kind". (Audubon, 1831-39, Vol. 1) While probably less common then in Audubon's day, nevertheless, breeding Pine Warblers can still be found in southeastern Pennsylvania, and as such, it would be entirely reasonable to encounter, both now and then, a recently fledged bird of this species during the month of May.

A number of noted Audubon scholars have offered their thoughts as to why Audubon ordered the composite plates produced. "In 1838, at the very end of the project, Audubon decided to correct all his past mistakes in bird identification by printing all the different, duplicated images of the same species onto the same print." (Steiner, 2003) "Audubon also ordered thirteen composite plates to correct errors he now perceived in his work. This usually meant transferring a bird or birds which Audubon had misidentified in one plate to the plate in which the birds were correctly identified." (Low, 2002) One fault, however, lies with this analysis. If one adheres to the belief that one of the purposes of creating the composite plates was to correct identification errors, then more than 13 composite plates should have been produced.

In 1829 Audubon painted a female Black-throated Blue Warbler which later became the subject of plate CXLVIII (and bore the name Pine Swamp Warbler). In plate CLV, Audubon provides his subscribers with the male of the species. In describing this plate, Susanne Low writes: "Audubon did not realize that the two females he painted for CXLVIII were Black-throated Blues; nor did Alexander Wilson. Wilson thought he had a new species, and called it Pine Swamp Warbler; Audubon followed along. Later, when painting a male for plate CLV, Audubon identified the bird correctly." (Low, 2002) Another example of an acknowledged identification error can be found in plate CXLV which depicts a male and female Palm Warbler (bearing the name Yellow Red-Poll Warbler on the plate). This same species was later illustrated in plate CLXIII. In his description of the Yellow Red-Poll Warbler, Audubon acknowledges "the error under which I laboured many years, in believing that this species and the *Sylvia palmarum* of Bonaparte, are distinct from each other. To the sound judgment of my good friend John Bachman, I am indebted for convincing me that the figure given by Prince of Musignano is that of our present bird, at a different period of life, and therefore with different plumage. I was not fully aware of this, until the 63d plate of my second volume of Illustrations had been delivered to the subscribers, bearing on it the name of *Sylvia palmarum.* That plate, however, will prove useful, as it represents both sexes of the Sylvia *petechia* in full summer plumage, while the 45th plate shews them in their first autumnal dress." (Audubon, 1831-39, Vol. 2) Audubon's identification confusion wasn't limited to song birds. Described as distinct species in Volume 1 of *Ornithological Biography* were the Pigeon Hawk (Plate XCII) and Petit Caporal (Plate LXXV) which are what we now know as the Merlin. In Volume V of *Ornithological Biography*, Audubon wrote a 209 page addendum titled *Appendix: Comprising Additional Observations on the Habits, Geographical Distribution, and Anatomical Structure of the Birds Described In This*

Work; Together with Corrections of Errors Relative to the Species. "The bird represented in the last-mentioned plate, and described under the name *Falco temerarious*, was merely a beautiful adult of the Pigeon Hawk, *F. columbarius*. That figure, and the two of the same species in Plate XCII, will afford a good opportunity of judging of the differences, as to size and colour, that occur in this species. The great inferiority of size of the individual represented as *F. temerarious*, was the cause of my mistaking it for a distinct species; and I have pleasure in stating that the Prince of Musignano was the first person who pointed out my error to me soon after the publication of my first volume." (Audubon, 1831-39, Vol. 5) [7] One is thus left to ask, why did Audubon not also order the production of composite plates to correct these admitted errors? [8]

---

[7] The incidents of admitted identification error described here are not unique. A number of errors involving identification and mis-communication with Havell occurred also in the production of plates L, CXXIII and CXCVIII which involve portrayal of the Magnolia and Swainson's Warblers. Audubon explains in detail the nature of these errors in detail in Volume 1 of *Ornithological Biography.*
In the Appendix of Volume 5 of *Ornithological Biography*, Audubon noted and corrects the following additional errors, all of which involved birds he described in Volume 1:
Plate LVI (Red-Shouldered Hawk) and Plate LXXI (Winter Hawk), both are plate depict Red-shouldered Hawks, the later being an immature.
Plate X (Brown Titlark) and Plate LXXX (Prairie Titlark) are American Pipits
Plate XCV (Yellow-Poll Warbler) and Plate XXXV (Children's Warbler) represent adult and immature Yellow Warblers respectively.
Plate XLVIII (Azure Warbler) and Plate XLIX (Blue-Green Warbler) also depict the adult and immature of the Cerulean Warbler.
After writing the five volumes of *Ornithological Biography*, Audubon produced a single volume titled *A Synopsis of the Birds of North America,* which was published in 1839. In a series of letters written between the Fall of 1838 and Spring of 1839, Audubon discusses the laying of the ground work for the *Synopsis*, which he completes in June, 1839. Since the written authorizations to Havell ordering the production of composite plates are dated August and September, 1838, it's evident that the writing of the *Synopsis* and the production of the composite plates occurred during the same time period. In the *Synopsis*, Audubon notes four additional errors:
Plate CCCLXVIII (Rock Ptarmigan) and Plate CCCCXVIII (American Ptarmigan). Both plates portray Rock Ptarmigans.
Plate CCCLXVI (Iceland or Jer Falcon) and Plate CXCVI (Labrador Falcon) Both plates depict Gyrfalcons.
Plate CCCLXX (American Water Ouzel) and Plate CCCCXXXV (contains two birds bearing the names Columbian Water Ouzel and Arctic Water Ouzel). The birds in these plates are American Dippers.
Plate XCIX and Plate CCCCXXIV depict the Brown-headed Cowbird, the latter plate being that of an immature male bird.

[8] There exist a number of other identification errors in *Birds of America* that have been well documented by Audubon scholars. For the purpose of this discussion, the authors are only concerned with those errors which were recognized and acknowledged by Audubon PRIOR to the completion of the composite plates at the end of the project.

Re-configured Plates

It has been an article of faith amongst Audubon scholars that as originally envisioned, each species represented in *Birds of America* would "depict the male, female, and immature of each species **on the same plate**, although the inclusion of the immatures was not accomplished in every case." (Low, 2002) (emphasis added) If one examines the 1827 prospectus for *Birds of America* (a copy of which was included in Volume I of *Ornithological Biography*), while Audubon does state an intention that "In every instance where a difference of plumage exists between the sexes, both the Male and the Female have been represented; and the extraordinary changes which some species undergo in their progress from youth to maturity, have been depicted." (Audubon, 1831-39, Vol. 1) However, in giving specific details of his work to prospective subscribers, Audubon makes no commitment to place all sexes, age and plumage variations for each species on a single plate.

"The particulars of the plans of the work may be reduced to the following heads:

1. The size of the work is Double Elephant Folio, the paper being of the finest quality.

2 . The engravings are, in every instance, of the exact dimensions of the drawings, which, without any exception, represent the birds and other objects of their natural size.

3. The Plates are colored in the most careful manner, from the original drawings.

4. The work appears in Numbers, of which five are published annually, each Number consisting of five plates.

5. The price of each number is Two Guineas, payable on delivery."

(Audubon, 1831-39, Vol. 1)

Thus, the commonly held belief that *all* of the composite plates were produced to correct errors may in and of itself be an incorrect assumption. With the later group of composite prints, Audubon may simply have requested that these 10 plates be produced for no other purpose than to have his personal copy (and that of his close friends) prepared in a reorganized fashion. Support for this proposition can be found in two items written by Audubon. The first, written in 1831 in the introduction to Volume 1 of *Ornithological Biography* suggested of the logistical problems that would render a faithful systematic approach to publication impractical: "When this work is completed, and when the results of my observations have been duly weighed and arranged, I shall reduce the whole to an order corresponding with improvements recently made in ornithological science, and present to you a Synopsis of the Birds of the United States, including ordinal, generic and specific characters, with the distinctive habits of each species, and references to the descriptions of other writers." (Audubon, 1831-39, Vol. 1) The synopsis alluded to was in fact published as a single volume in 1839. In the preface to that publication, Audubon states: "The figures and descriptions contained in the works entitled 'The Birds of America' and 'Ornithological Biography, or an Account of the Habits of the Birds of the United States,' having been issued in the miscellaneous manner which was thought best adapted to the occasion, or which was rendered necessary by circumstances, seemed to require a systematic index, in which the nomenclature should be corrected, and the species arranged agreeably to my present views." (Audubon, 1839) The following from individual entries in the *Ornithological Biography* for some of the species which are the subject of the composite plates add further credence to the above:

Baltimore Oriole – "The plumage of the male bird is not mature until the spring, and I have therefore in my drawing represented the males of the first, second, and third years. The female will form the subject of another plate. The male of the first year was taken for a female by my engraver, during my absence, and marked as such, although some of the plates were corrected the moment I saw the mistake." (Audubon, 1831-39, Vol. 1)[9]

Blackburnian Warbler – "The specimen from which I made the drawing copied in the plate before you…" Note the use of the singular. The very last sentence in this entry, added almost as an afterthought, states "The female resembles the male in colouring, but the bright orange of the head and breast is replaced by yellow." (*Ibid.*, Vol. 2)[10]

Wilson's Plover - On Plate CCLXXXIV, two Purple Sandpipers are depicted along with a Wilson's Plover. Audubon made a notation in his original Purple Sandpiper painting requesting that Havell add the Plover. While Audubon states in the *Ornithological Biography* regarding the Wilson's Plover that plate (CCIX) depicts a female and a "Young Male in winter plumage….The Adult Male is represented in Plate 284." (*Ibid.*, Vol. 3) Interestingly, the plover on the sandpiper plate is not identified by its common name in the legend, suggesting that the inclusion of this bird was purely for aesthetic purposes.[11]

---

[9] The Baltimore Oriole plate (XII), was published in 1827, four years prior to Volume 1 of the *Ornithological Biography*, thus adding further evidence to argue that early in the project, Audubon made an intentional decision to allow sex or plumage variations in specific species to be depicted on separate plates. [For a thorough discussion on the dates of publication of Audubon's work, see: Stone, W. 1906. A Bibliography and Nomenclator of the Ornithological Works of John James Audubon. Auk, 23: 298-312.]

[10] By combining the Blackburnian Warbler prints into one, Audubon almost, but not quite, got it right. Plate CXXXIV, the Hemlock Warbler, Audubon believed to be a distinct species. The two birds depicted in this plate are also female Blackburnians.

[11] Low states that the image of the Wilson's Plover in the Purple Sandpiper plate and the female in plate CCIX are identical birds. The authors, in examining these plates in detail, noted numerous differences, including a clear difference in the positioning of the tail feathers. Thus, while the posture of both birds is similar, it does not appear that these two prints depict an identical bird. It may well be

Sanderling – "My plate of this species represents two birds in winter plumage, which were obtained in East Florida in the month of December. The figure of a fine male,   which, being on another sheet of paper, was overlooked during my absence from London, you will find in Plate CCLXXXV of 'The Birds of America'." (*Ibid.*, Vol. 3)[12] The image of the Sanderling in breeding plumage (which also depicts a Sabine's Gull) was apparently originally painted by Audubon on a separate piece of paper, "intending it for CCXXX, but which had inadvertently been left off." (Low, 2002) Thus, any error that occurred was in fact that of Havell in the production process and not one of identification by Audubon.

Louisiana Tanager (Western Tanager) – "Wilson was the first ornithologist who figured this handsome bird. From this time until the return of Dr. Townsend from the Columbia River no specimen seems to have been procured. That gentlemen forwarded several males…Some of these I purchased, and, on his return to Philadelphia, I was presented with a female…which you will find in Plate CCCC, fig. 4. The only account of this species is by Thomas Nuttall, who, however, was unacquainted with the female." (*Ibid.,* Vol. 4)

Evening Grosbeak – "In the present plate you will find the figure of a male only; but in Plate CCCCXXIV, are representations of the young male and adult female, which however are described here." (*Ibid.*, Vol. 4)

Bullock's Troopial (Bullock's Oriole) – Plate CCCLXXXVIII, as published depicted six birds, a male Tricolored Blackbird, a male, female

that a more comprehensive comparison of these prints, side-by-side with the original painting will clarify this issue.

[12] The Sanderling plate first appeared in 1834 and bore the name Ruddy Plover. Audubon, however, identifies this species as Sanderling in Volume 3 of *Ornithological Biography* which book bears the date of December 1, 1835 in the preface. As the composite plates weren't produced until 1838, the name Sanderling is that which is found on the composite plates.

and immature Yellow-headed Blackbirds and a male Bullock's Oriole. Thomas Nuttall originally provided Audubon with the specimen and his notes on the later species. Thereafter, Audubon "received another from Dr. Townsend, along with a female and a young male, both of which I have figured in Plate CCCCXXXIII." (*Ibid.,* Vol. 5)

Lazuli Finch (Lazuli Bunting) – Audubon included the male of this species as one of three species portrayed on Plate CCCXCVIII. The female was included on Plate CCCCXXIV. At the time when Audubon painted these birds, he had in his possession both the male and female; "It has been my good fortune to procure a fine pair from Dr. Townsend, who shot them on the Columbia River, on the 3d of June, 1836, so that I have been enabled to represent the female, which has not hitherto been figured, as well as the male." (*Ibid.,* Vol. 5)

The two additional plates not discussed above and which comprise the balance of our second group of composite plates are:

Plate CVII which depicts two Canada Jays (Gray Jays), to which was added an immature from Plate CCCCXIX.

Plate CCCLXIX originally contained a male Mountain Mocking bird (Sage Thrasher) and two Varied Thrushes. A female Varied Thrush was added from Plate CCCCXXXIII.

The net conclusion one can arrive at from the above is that given the pressures and difficulties involved in bringing his work to its ulti-mate fruition, Audubon was forced as a matter of necessity to allow a limited number of plates to go into production that failed to contain all of the various sex and plumage differences. Even though Audubon knew that some of the plates were less than complete, in order to meet the production schedule Audubon and Havell were trying to keep, compromises had to be made. Thus, the birds which were combined to form the second group of composite plates may have been separated initially as part of practical business decisions or simple production errors.[13]

---

[13] For a through understanding of the logistical obstacles encountered by Audubon, the reader is encouraged to consult any of the recent biographies published about Audubon and referenced elsewhere in this publication.

Timeline of Events Surrounding the Production of the Composite Plates

1838

June 20, 1838 – The first print of Plate 435 is pulled by Havell in London.

Summer, 1838 – Audubon and William MacGillivray are engaged in the completion of Volumes 4 and 5 of *Ornithological Biography*

July 1, 1838 – Audubon in Edinburgh sends a letter to his son, John Woodhouse Audubon wherein he notes that Volume 4 of *Ornithological Biography* will go to press on July 2, 1838.

August 20, 1838 – The first letter from John James Audubon and his son, Victor Gifford, is sent from Edinburgh to Havell in London requesting the composite plates be printed.

August 28, 1838 – The second letter from Victor Gifford Audubon in Edinburgh is sent to Havell in London authorizing the production of the composites plates.

September 15, 1838 – Audubon and his family, in the company of MacGillivray leave Edinburgh on a short tour of highlands of Scotland.

September 26, 1838 – The third letter regarding the composite plates is sent by Victor Gifford Audubon from Edinburgh to Havell in London.

1839

January, 1839 – Victor Gifford Audubon returns to America.

February, 1839 (approximately) – Havell begins the process of disposing of his stock and the dismantling his printing shop at 77 Oxford Street, London, in advance of his immigration to America.

May 1, 1839 – Volume 5 of *Ornithological Biography* is completed and sent to press.

July 1, 1839 – Audubon in Edinburgh presents a personalized copy of *Ornithological Biography* to MacGillivray

Early September, 1839 – Audubon arrives in America.

September 15, 1839 – Havell arrives in New York

Production Process

While volumes have been written about the history and mechanical processes used to produce the 435 plates of *Birds of America*, little attention has been directed to the 13 composite plates and the unique features contained therein that distinguish them from the thousands of the more familiar prints that were produced by Havell. To understand some of these differences, the printing process utilized to produce the prints for *Birds of America* must first be discussed. As Audubon intended to depict each species in life size, the paper used in the printing process (known as double elephant folio) was the largest then available, measuring 29 1/2" X 39 1/2". The cotton rag paper was purchased by Havell from one of two esteemed English paper manufacturers. The paper from both mills bore one of two watermarks, either "J. Whatman" or "J. Whatman Turkey Mill" and included a date. One commentator has stated that the "presence of a Whatman watermark is the single most important factor for authenticating a Havell print." (Steiner, 2003) However, because many prints over the years have been trimmed to accommodate framing, it is not uncommon to encounter a genuine print that is missing the watermark. Hence, a secondary characteristic of the printing process, the "plate mark", is often used to aid in the determination of authenticity. It is the creation of the "plate mark" during the printing process that provides some of the singular characteristics found in the composite prints.

The original Havell prints are often referred to as "engravings", "etchings" or "aquatints". In truth, each of these terms represents a discrete technique in the *intaglio* printing process. Simply, *intaglio* printing involved a basic four-step process. The first involved tracing onto thin paper from Audubon's original paintings, the species to be depicted. The second step requires that the traced image be transposed onto a copper plate. Using a combination of engraving, etching and aquatint, Havell would cut into the surface of the copper plate, the desired image.

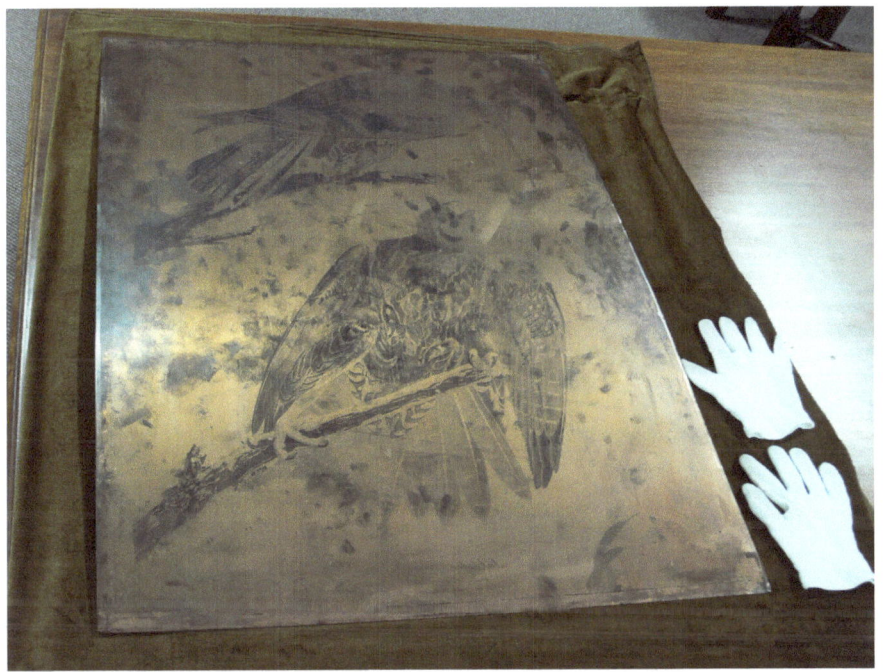

1. - Original copper plate Labrador Falcon (Gyrfalcon) #CXCVI . The size of the plate can be determined from the adult size gloves next to the plate.

A key point to remember is that the image has been cut below the surface of the copper plate. After the copper plate has been fully en-graved, it is inked with black ink and then the surface of the copper plate cleaned, leaving the ink only on that part of the copper plate that has been incised below the surface. The third step requires that the paper sheet that is to be printed be wetted and then, under pressure, pressed onto the copper plate. The result is an inked image that sits on top of the paper. After the paper has dried, a team of colorists working by hand would apply the finished coloring, completing the last step in the printing process. To achieve the realism and accuracy necessary in a project of this magnitude, a "hand-painted master proof, or coloring guide, was then worked up for the artist's approval, to be used as a 'pattern' to be copied by the colorist." (Goddu, 2002)

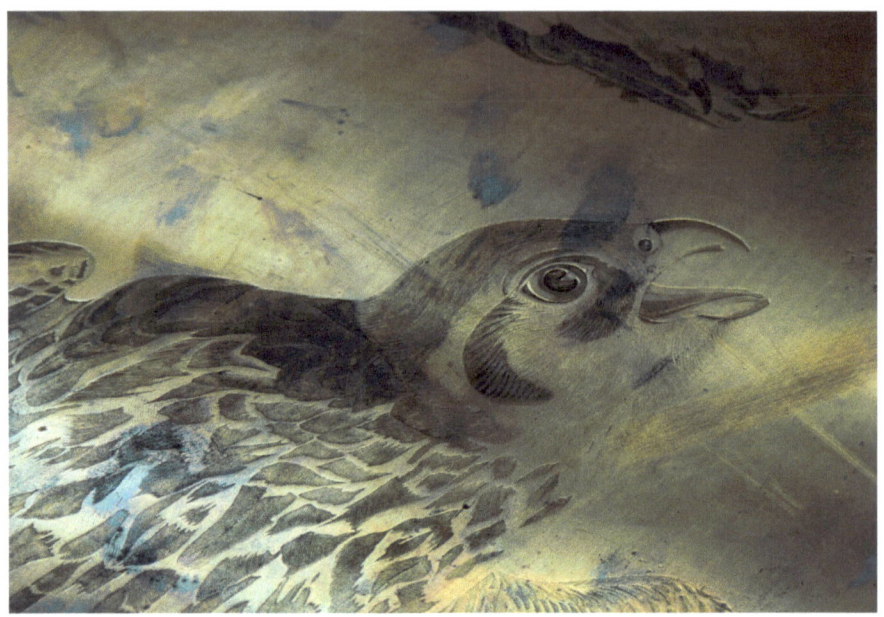

2. - Detail of original copper printing plate Labrador Falcon (Gyrfalcon) #CXCVI .

Because the black ink image from the copper plate is transferred to paper under the enormous pressure of the press, the resultant print is surrounded by a visible rectangular "plate mark" which was created where the paper extended beyond the edges of the copper plate. Because Audubon's paintings (from which the prints were produced) tended to fall roughly into three size categories the resulting prints and corresponding "plate mark" fell into three size categories as well. The largest of Audubon's paintings (and the resulting prints), fill the paper almost entirely. In the second category were medium size images which resulted in a "plate mark" that measured approximately 21" X 26". In the last category are the small images, whose "plate mark" measures about 12" X 19". Because the composite prints were created from separate copper plates, one can observe, on close examination, the overlapping "plate marks".

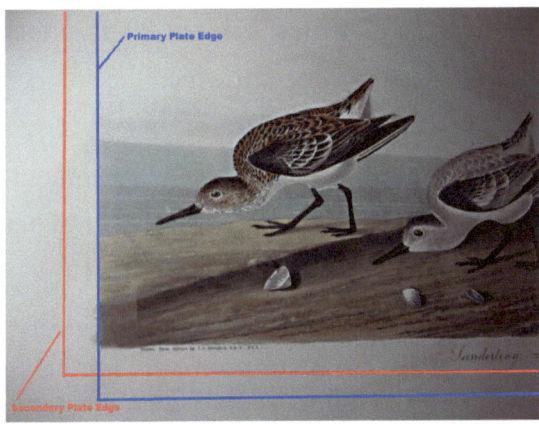

3. - Detail of the Sanderling Composite plate highlighting the two "plate marks"

4. - Detail of the lower left corner of Sanderling composite plate showing the two "plate marks" visible with a strong raking light.

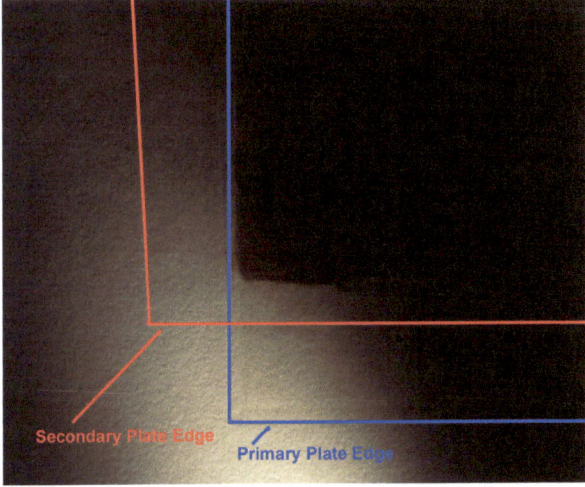

5. - Same picture as above with platemarks highlighted.

With the exception of plates XII and CVII, which are medium sized images, the primary plates from which the composites were created are small sized prints. While other researchers have systematically documented the size of the "plate marks" on the common 435 prints, to these authors' knowledge, no one has undertaken the analysis of the plate marks on the composite prints. Hence, this study endeavors to depict and describe for the first time the location and size of the "plate marks" created by Havell during the process of producing the composite plates.

Mechanically, the composite plates involved the inking of only a small portion of the copper plate that contained the added image (the "secondary" plate) and than the pressing of that copper plate off center over the previously printed "primary" plate, thus creating the combined composite. In printing the composite plates, Havell retained the original bird depictions and all of the original numbering and attribution information contained in the "primary" plate. Only the added bird (and in some cases a limited amount of background or foliage) was incorporated from the secondary plate. In adding the additional bird from the secondary plate to the primary plate, Havell in some cases had to remove or alter the background to accommodate the additional image. Hence, where the background on the composite plate differs markedly from the primary plate, those distinctions can be noted.

Composite Plates
Baltimore Oriole (Plate XII)

This composite print was created with the addition of a female from Plate CCCCXXXIII. The added bird is positioned in the upper left quadrant

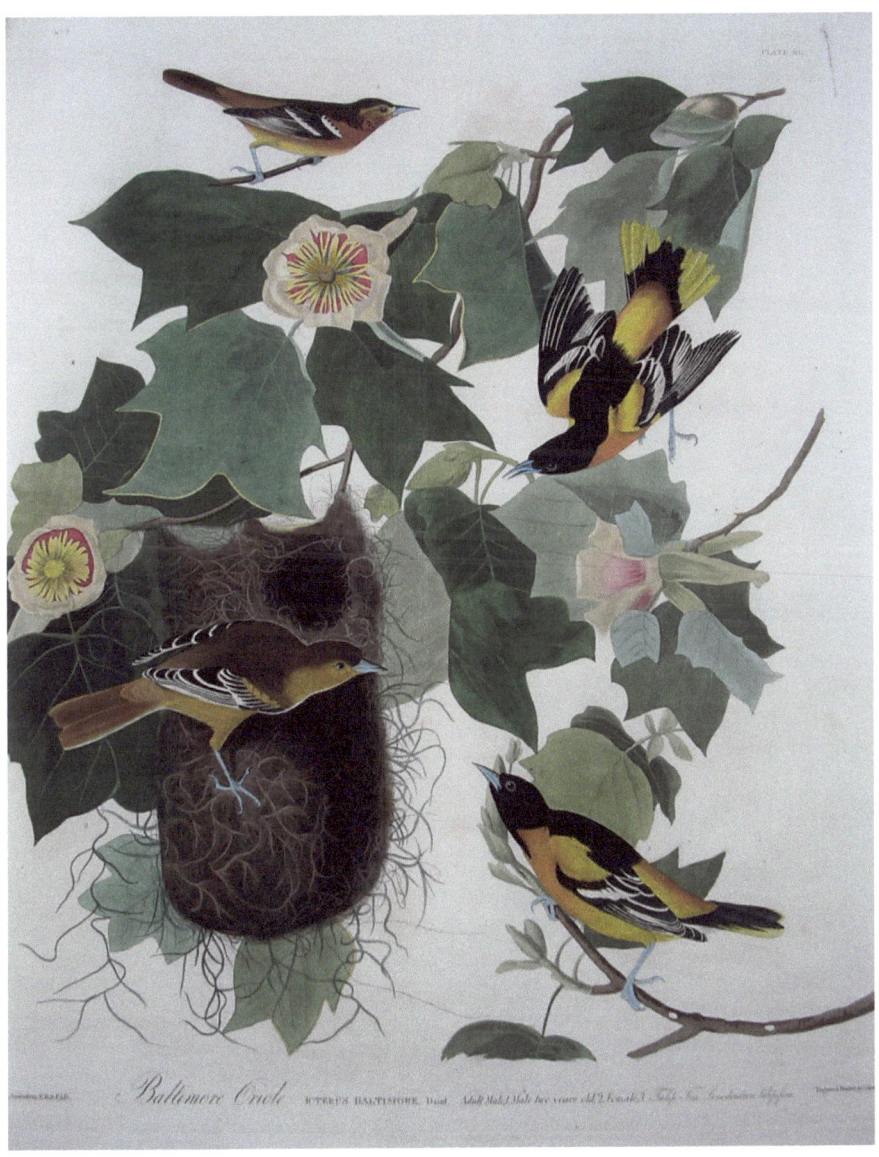

6. - Composite plate XII

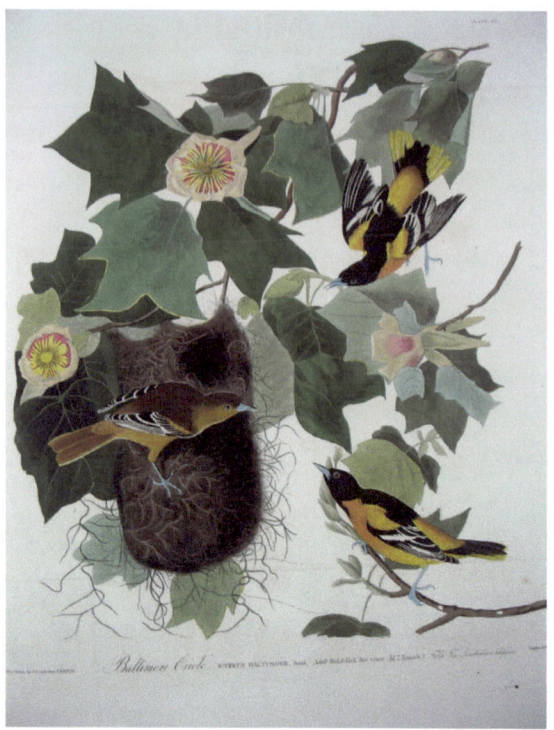

7. - Primary plate

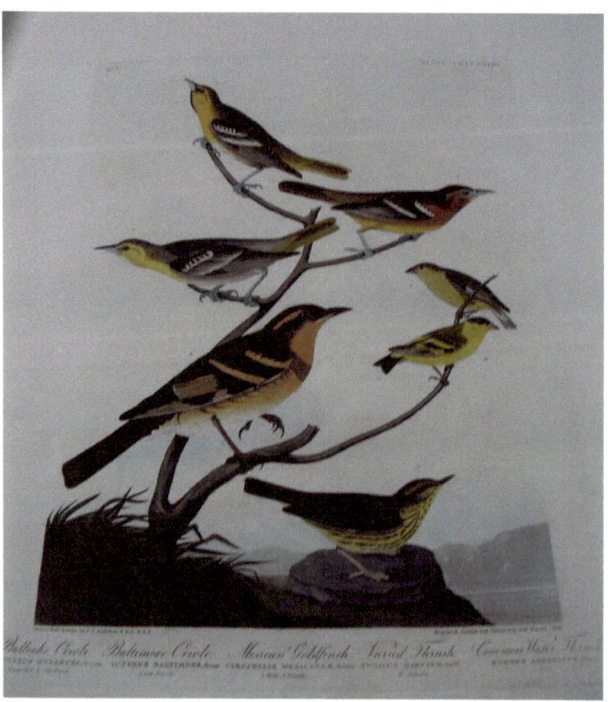

8. - Secondary plate

In order to create the composite, Havell removed a portion of the leaf that the added bird is now perched upon.

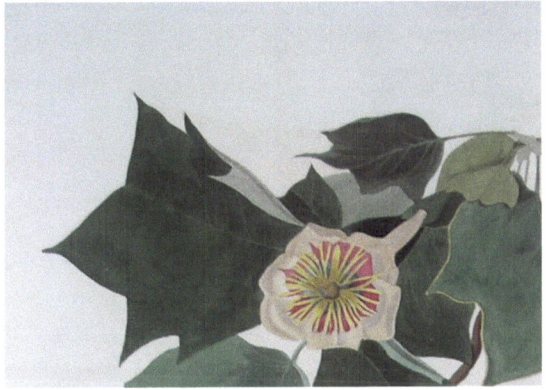

9. - Detail of the primary plate

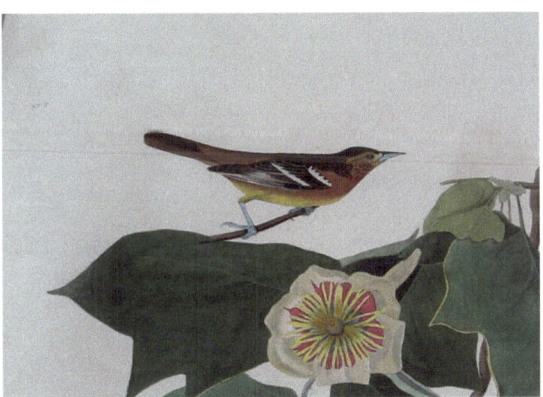

10. - Detail of the composite plate

The secondary plate mark is located 11 ¼" to the left and 4" above the primary plate mark. The horizontal plate marks for the secondary plate extend fully to the left edge of the paper and the left side vertical plate mark is not visible.

Maryland Yellow Throat or Yellow-breasted Warbler (Plate XXIII)

Now called the Common Yellowthroat, this composite was made with the addition of a male from Plate XXIV. The added image is located towards the top of the print, slightly left of center.

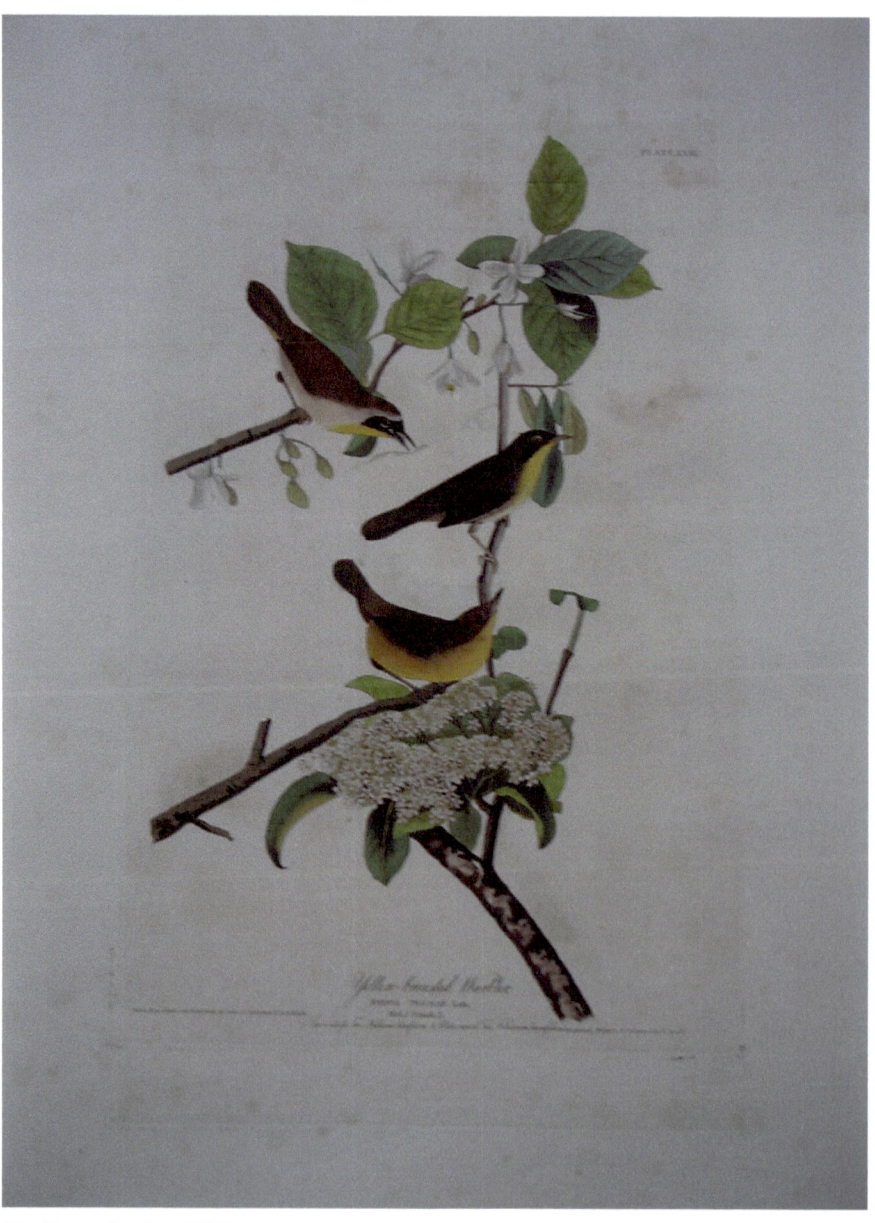

11. - Composite plate XXIII

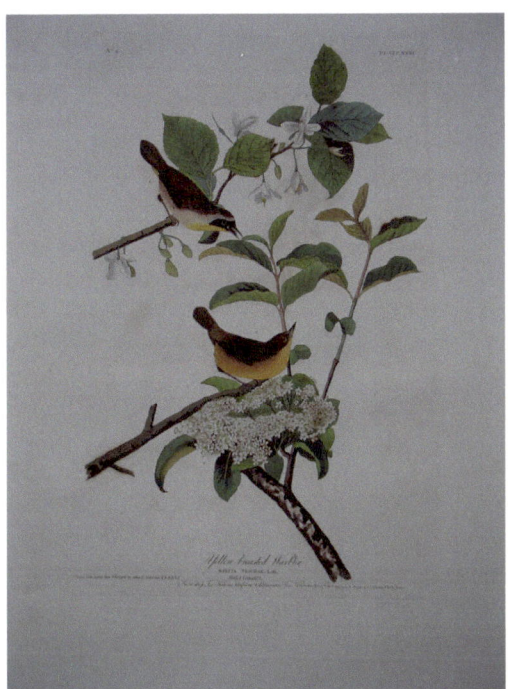

12. - Primary plate

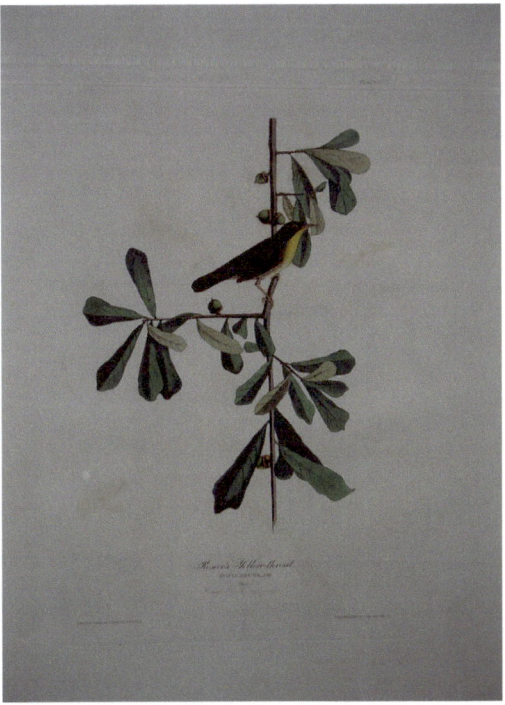

13. - Secondary plate

Where the new bird is positioned, foliage from the primary plate was removed, somewhat ineffectively. As can be noted, edges of the removed leaves can still be seen.

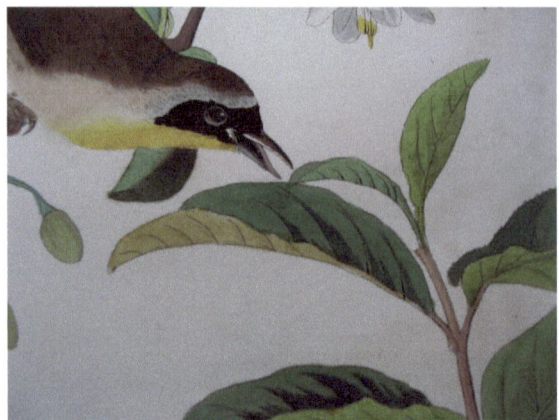

14. - Detail of the primary plate

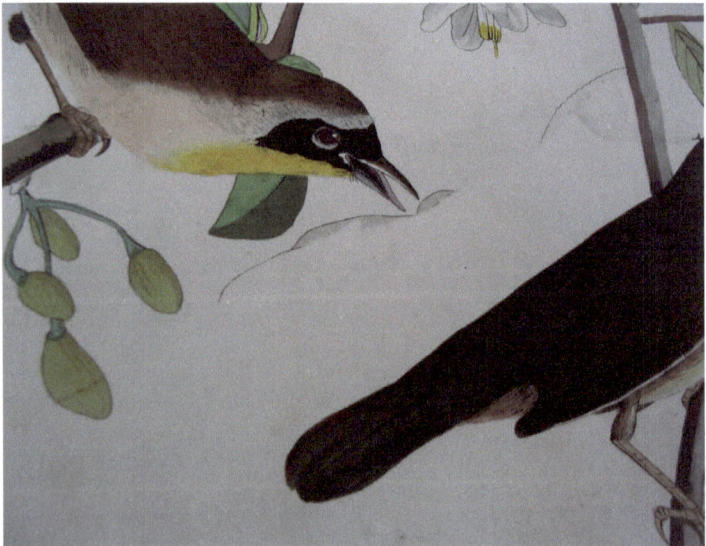

15. - Detail of the composite plate

In producing this composite, the secondary copper plate was positioned slightly askew in relation to the primary print. At the bottom, the secondary plate mark was measured 1/8" to the right of the primary plate mark, but at the top, the plate marks were flush with each other. The secondary plate mark horizontally is located 1 1/2" below the primary.

Canada Jay (Plate CVII)

Currently named the Gray Jay, an immature bird from Plate CCCCXIX was added image that created this composite plate. It is positioned in the upper left of the print. The added bird is sitting on a branch which appears to be effectively suspended in air.

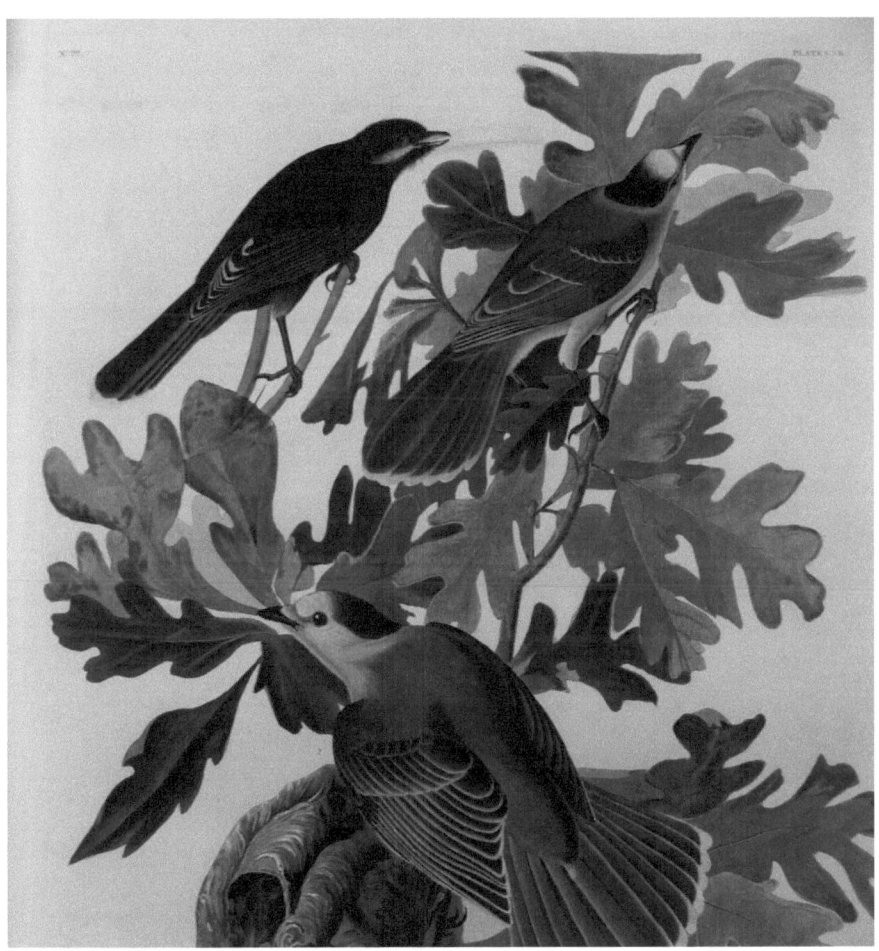

16. - Composite plate CVII

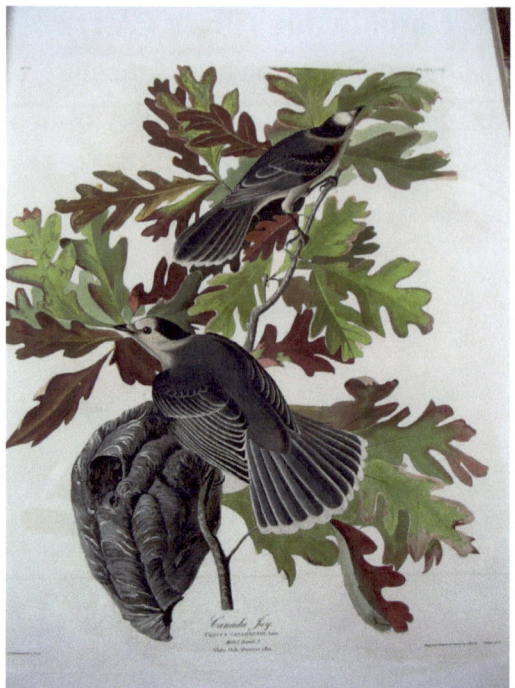

17. - Primary plate

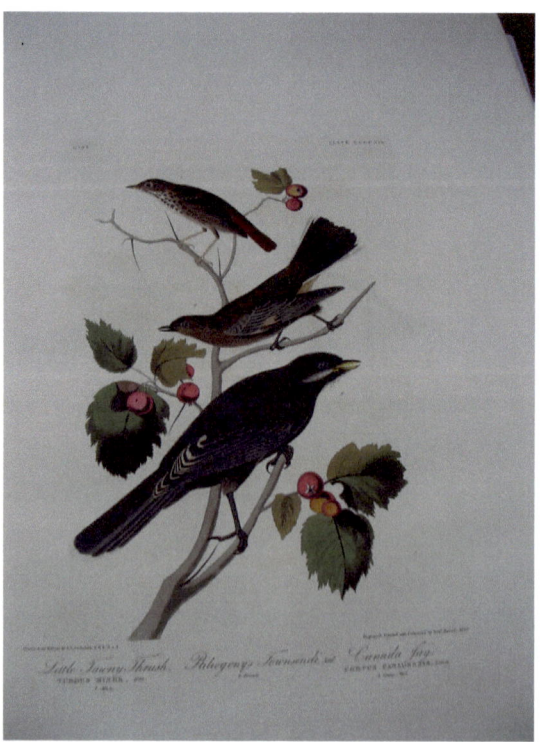

18. - Secondary plate

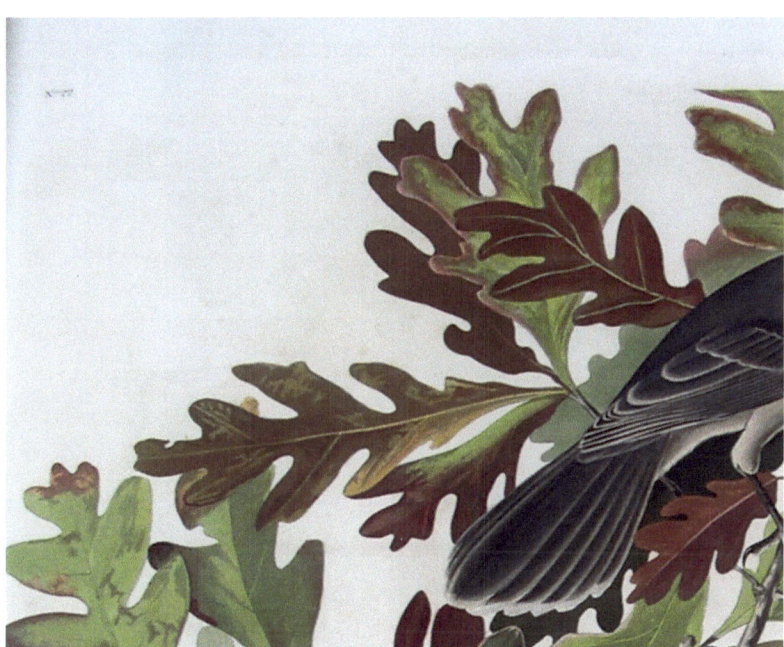

19. - Detail of primary plate

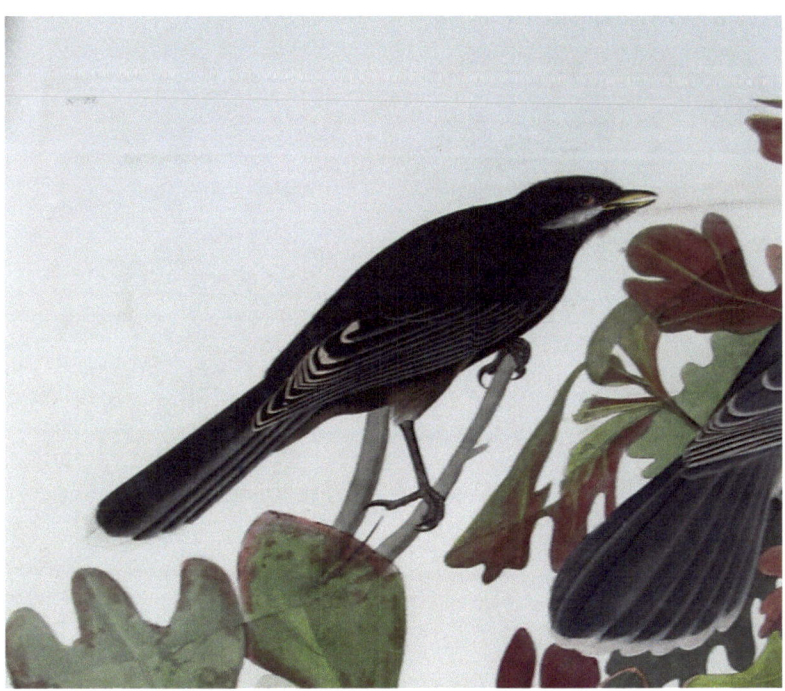

20. - Detail of composite plate

A close examination of the leaves below the added image shows a marked masking effect. The coloration of the background leaves is exceedingly uneven.

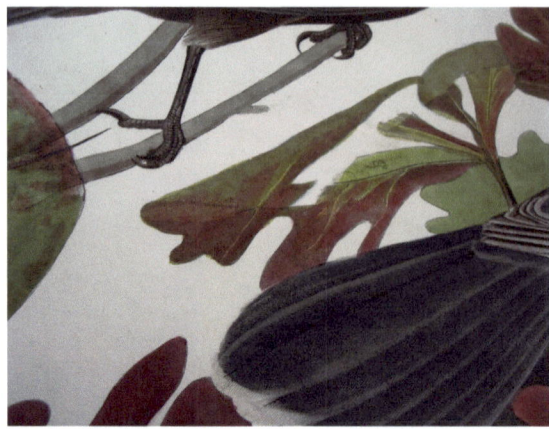

21. - Detail of composite plate

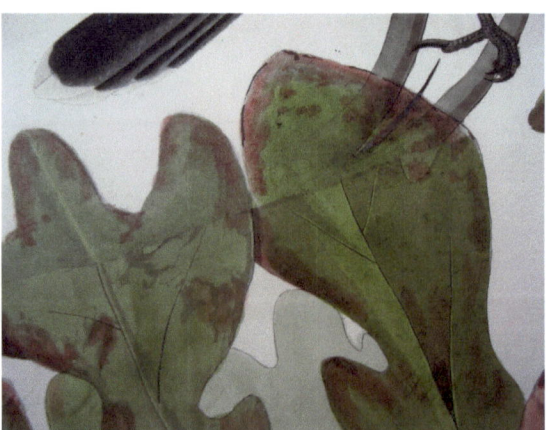

22. - Detail of composite plate

The image of the added bird as it appears on the secondary plate was markedly sharper then its counterpart on the composite. A possible explanation may be that by the time composite plate was produced, the secondary copper plate was suffering from wear.

The horizontal sides of the secondary plate mark are positioned 1 3/4" below the primary and the vertical edges are located 3/8" to the left of the primary plate marks.

Hooded Warbler (Plate CX)

The immature bird from Plate IX is positioned in the lower right quadrant to create this composite.

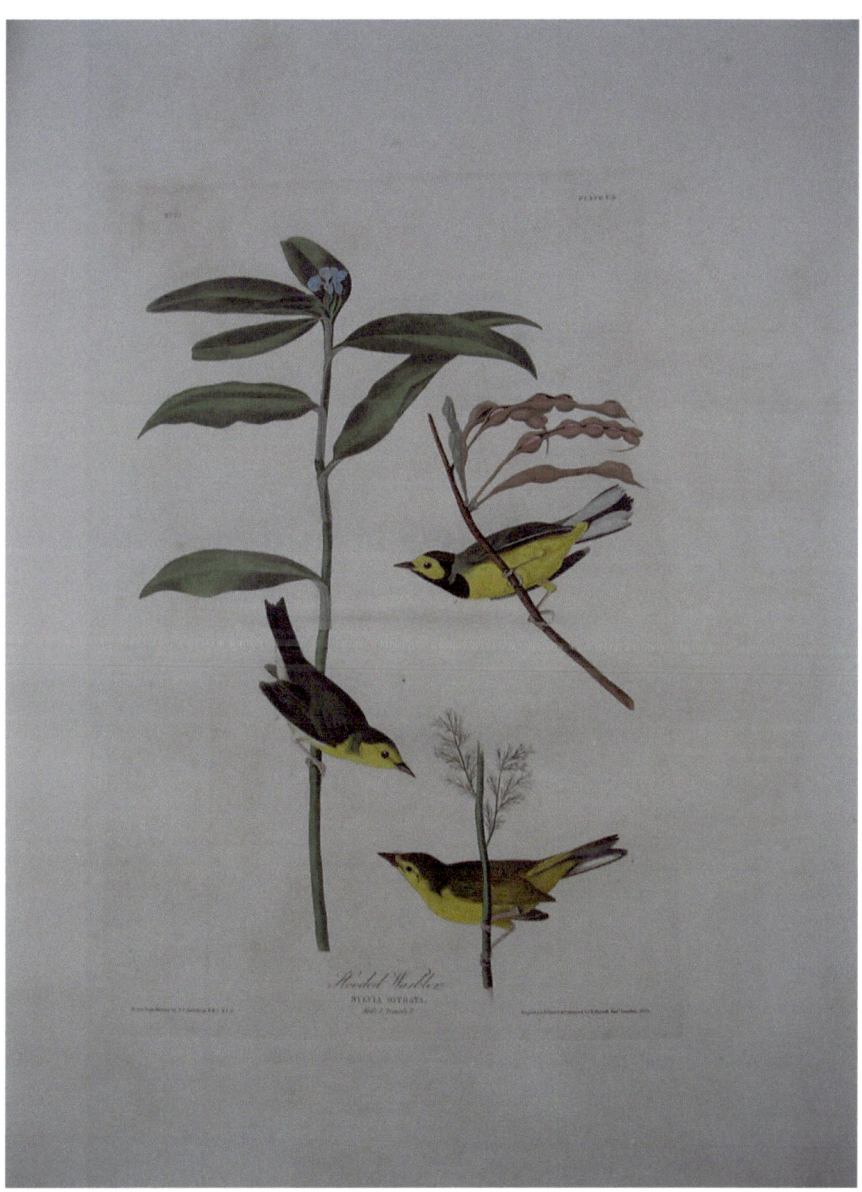

23. - Composite plate CX

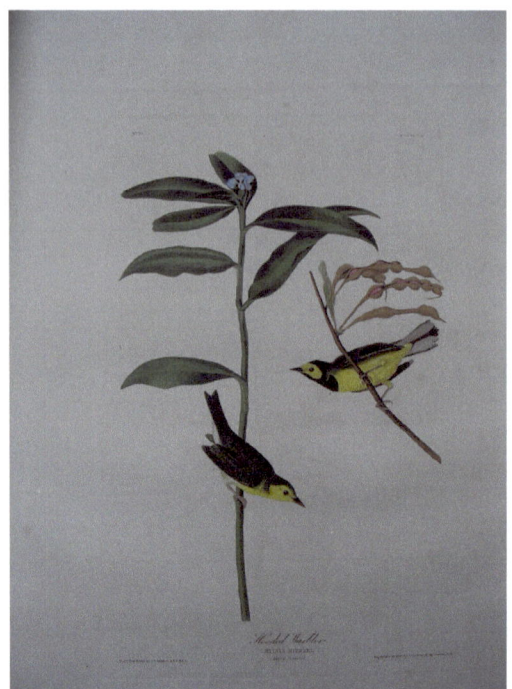

24. - Primary plate

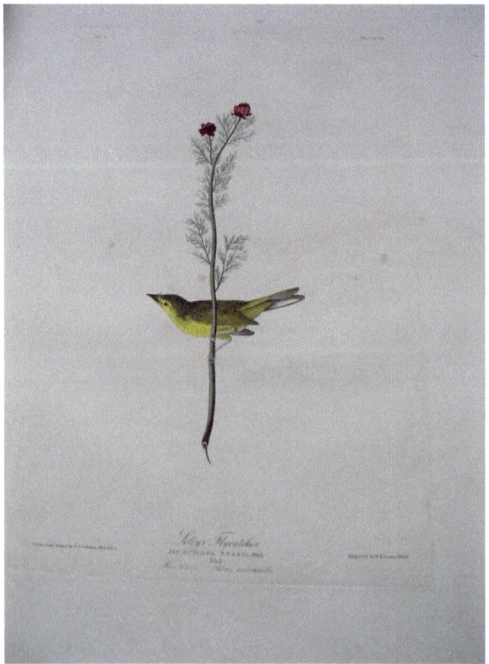

25. - Secondary plate

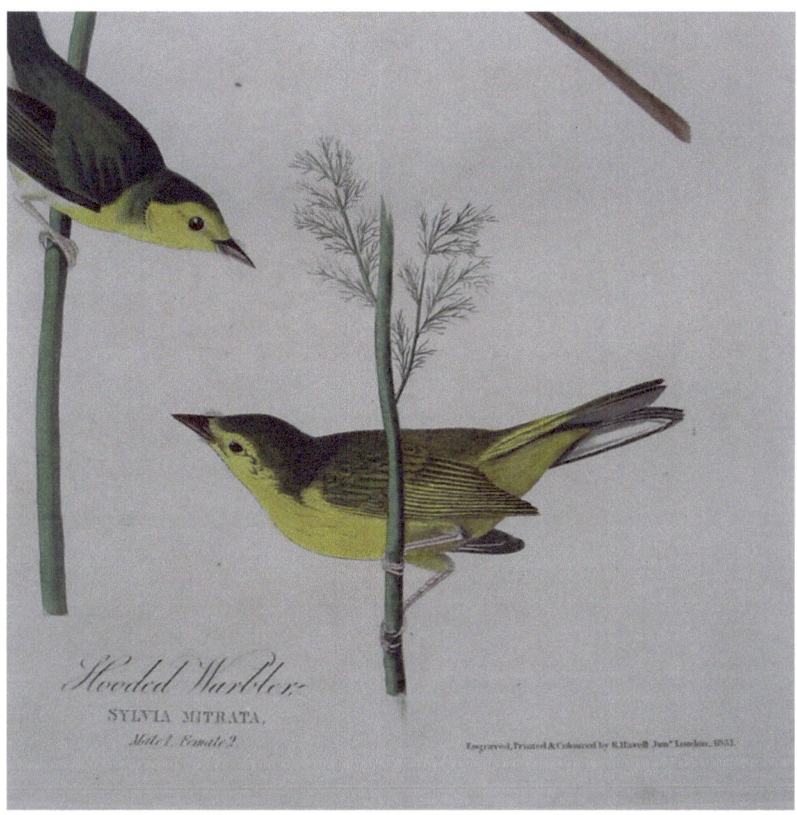

26. - Detail of composite plate

The secondary plate mark is located 2 ¼" to the right and 5 1/8" down from the primary plate mark.

Blackburnian Warbler (Plate CXXXV)

The female from Plate CCCXCIX was added in to this composite by placing her in the lower left quadrant of the primary.

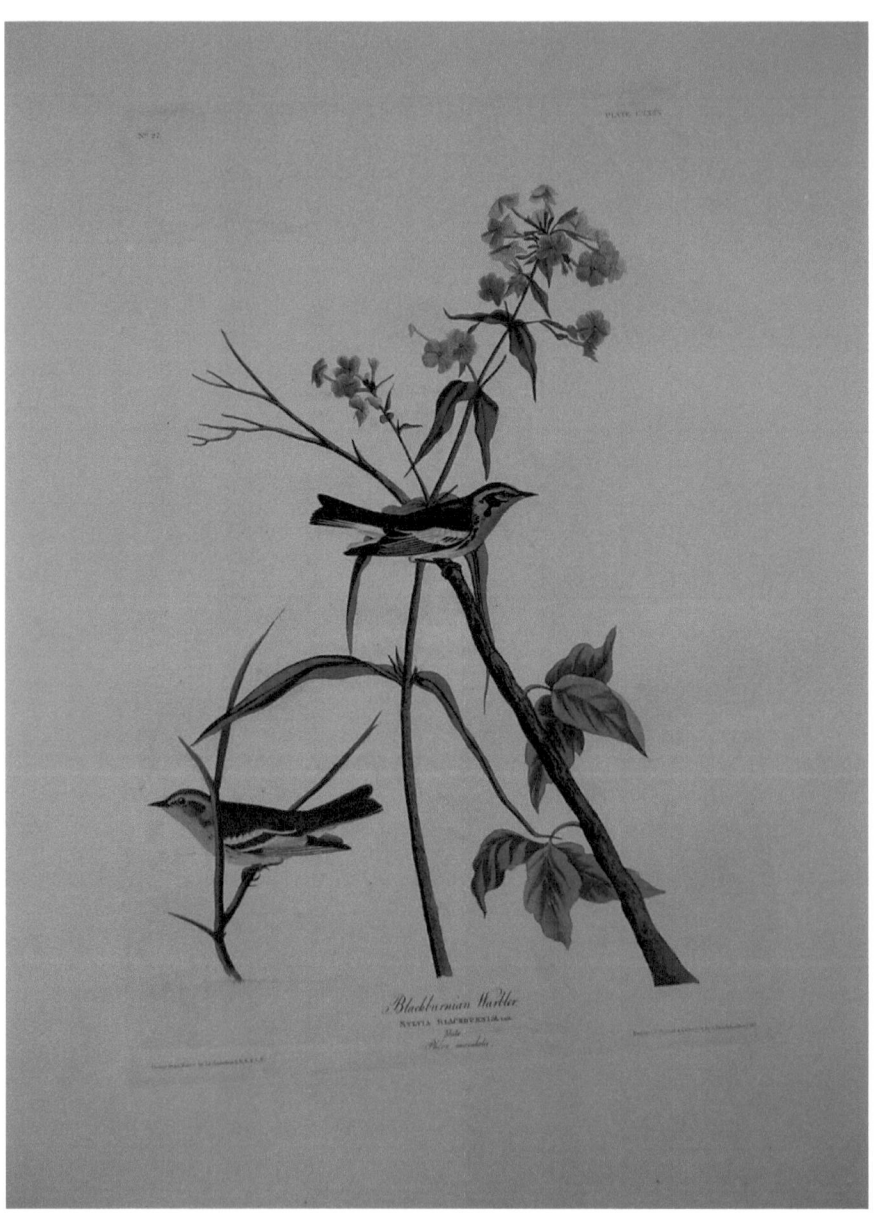

27. - Composite plate CXXXV

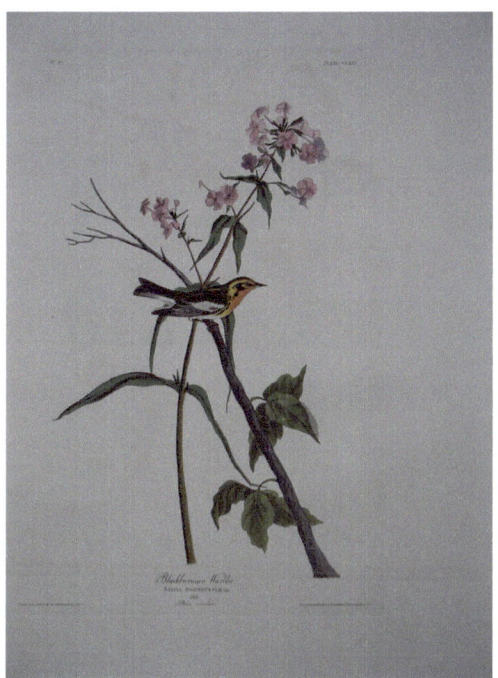

28. - Primary plate

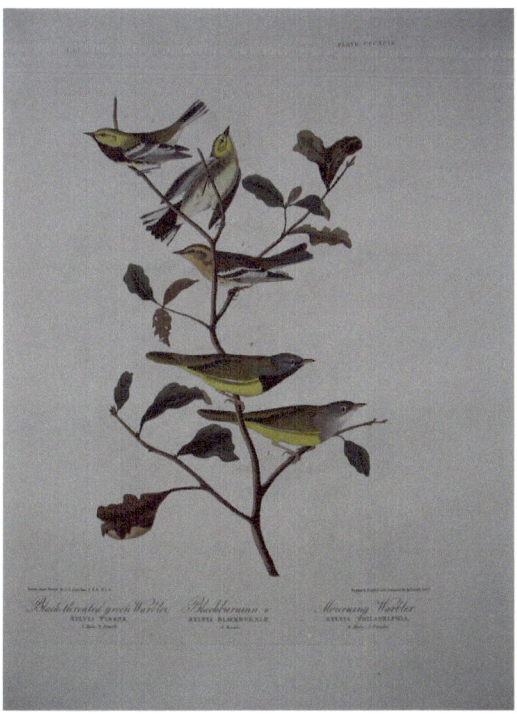

29. - Secondary plate

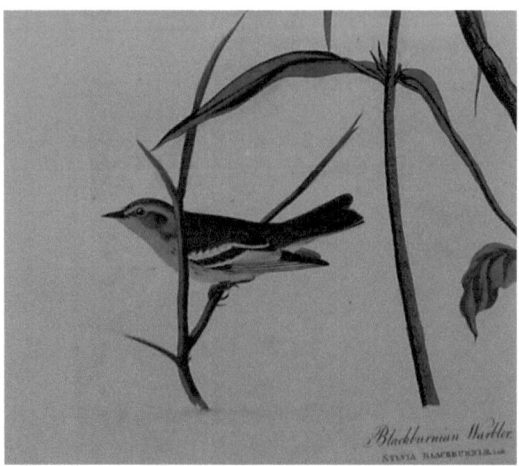

30. - Detail of composite plate

The plate marks created from the secondary copper plate are located 3 7/8" to the left and 6 5/8" down below the primary plate marks.

Pine Creeping Warbler (Plate CXL)

An immature Pine Warbler from Plate XXX is the added image in this composite. The bird is positioned centrally at top of the print.

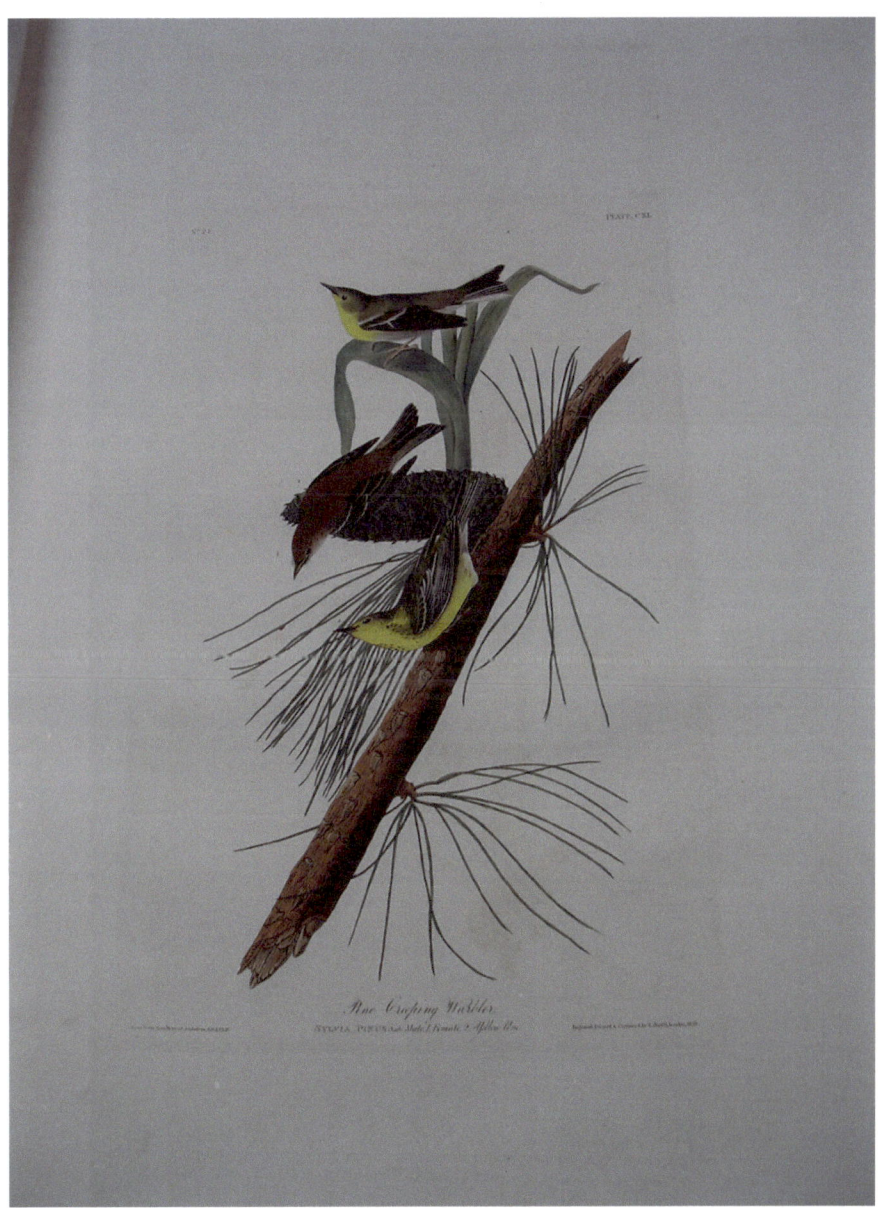

31. - Composite plate CXL

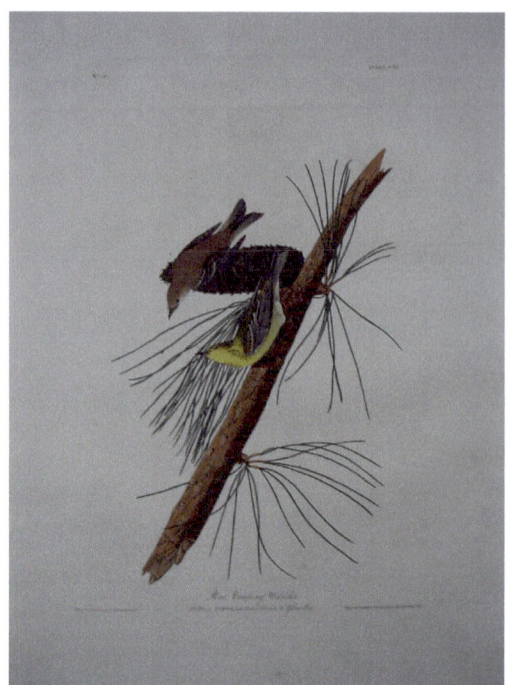

32. - Primary plate

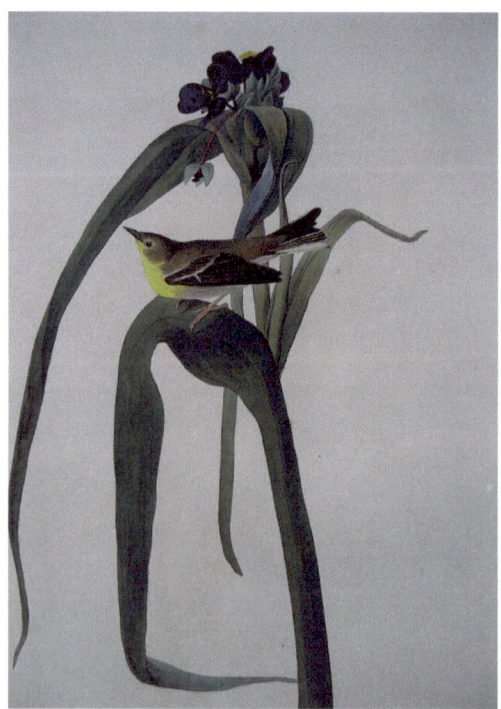

33. - Secondary plate

The leaves that the added bird is perching on appear to be completely redrawn, and not simply transposed from the secondary plate.

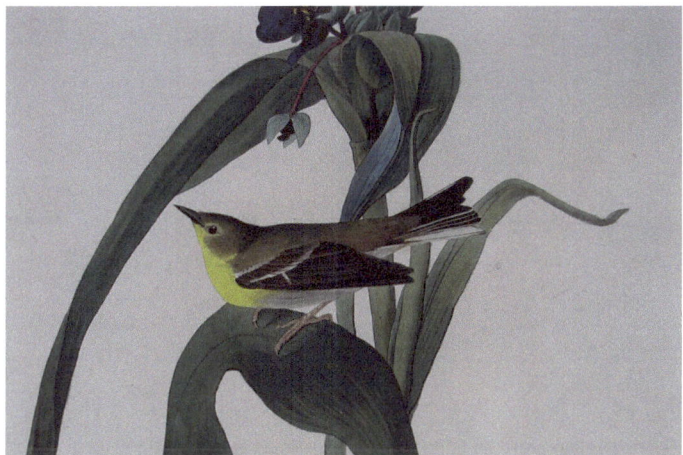

34. - Detail of secondary plate

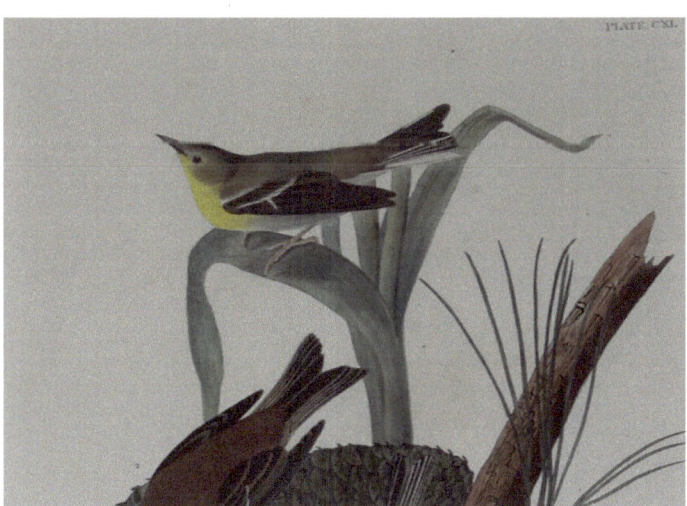

35. - Detail of composite plate

The vertical plate marks of the primary and secondary plates line up perfectly. The horizontal plate marks from the secondary are located 4 7/8" above the primary.

Wilson's Plover (Plate CCIX)

This composite was created by the addition of the Wilson's Plover from Plate CCLXXXIV, which is positioned in the lower right quadrant of the primary.

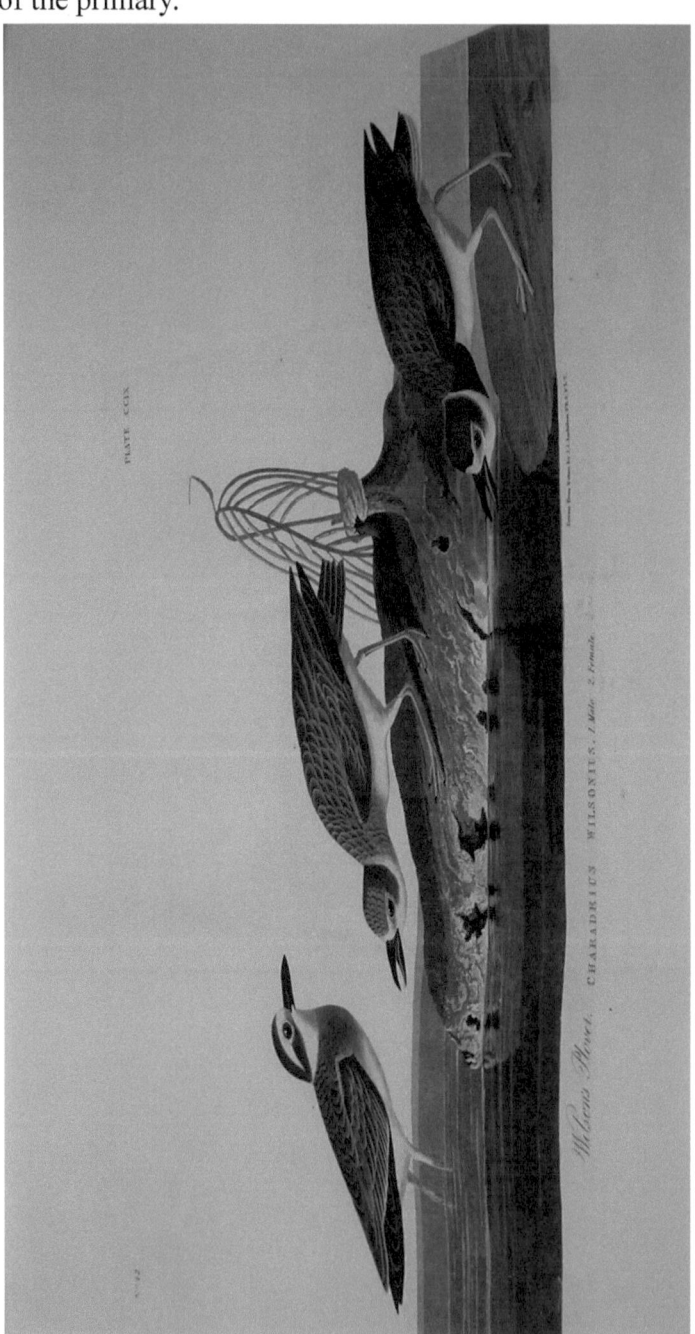

36. – Composite plate CCIX

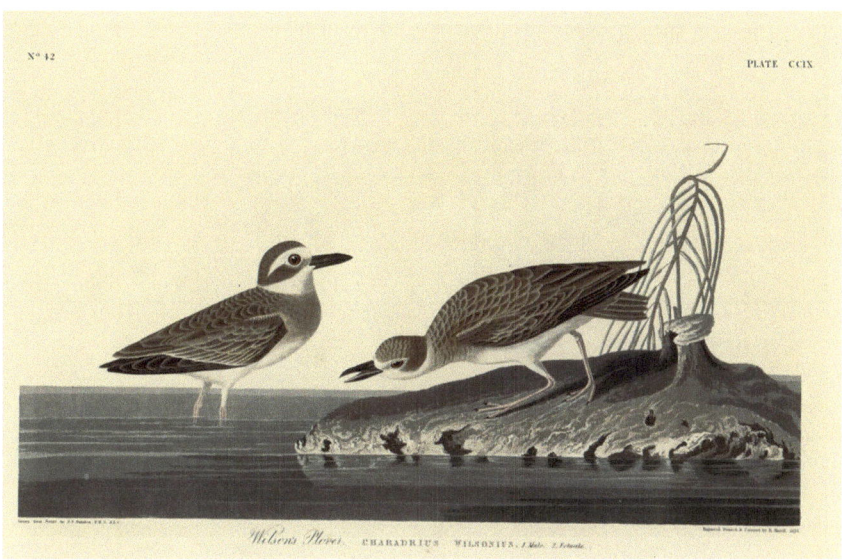

37. - Primary plate

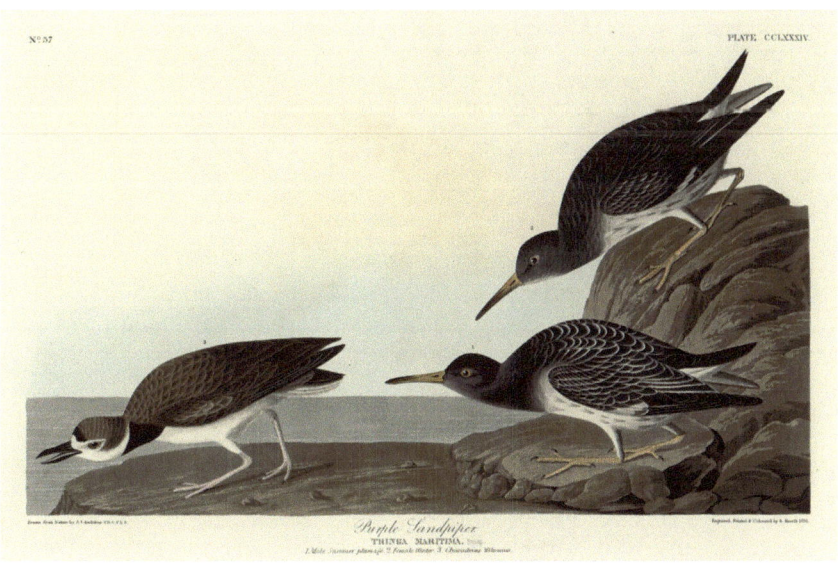

38. - Secondary plate

The mud flat depicted on the right side of the primary plate has been removed to accommodate the additional bird.

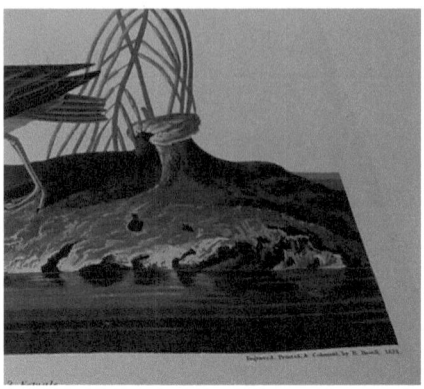

39. - Detail of primary plate

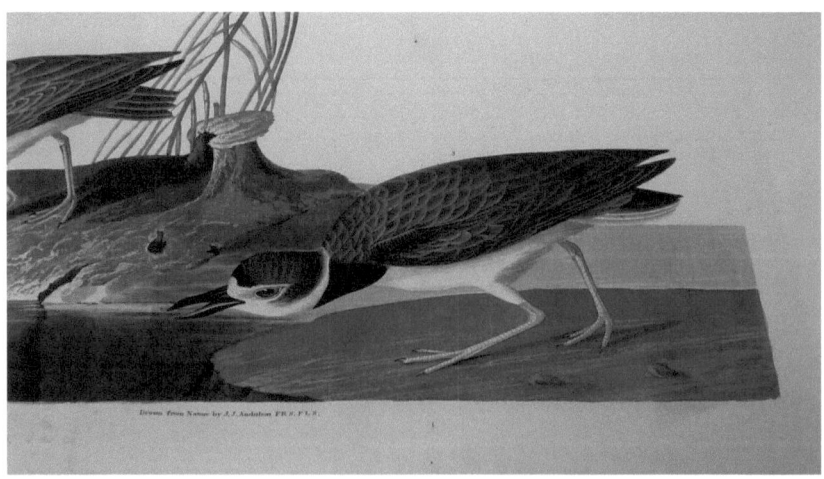

40. - Detail of composite plate

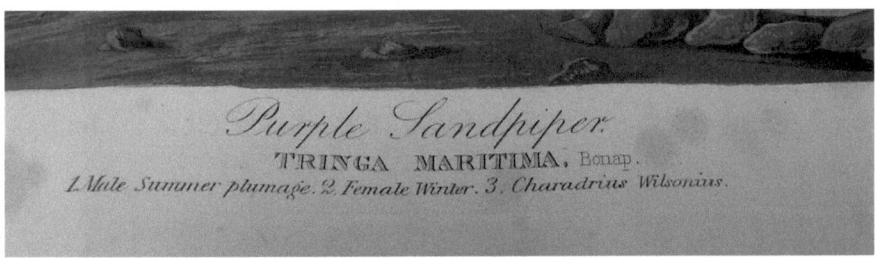

41. - Detail of secondary plate. Note that the Wilson's Plover on this print is not identified by its common name in the legend, suggesting that the inclusion of this bird was purely for aesthetic purposes

The horizontal plate marks of the primary and secondary are flush with each other and in the case of the secondary, extends entirely off the right side of the paper. The left side plate mark of secondary is located 4 ½" to the right of the corresponding primary plate mark.

Sanderling (Plate CCXXX)

In this composite print, the added image of the species in breeding plumage from Plate CCLXXXV is positioned to the left of the images depicted in the primary plate.

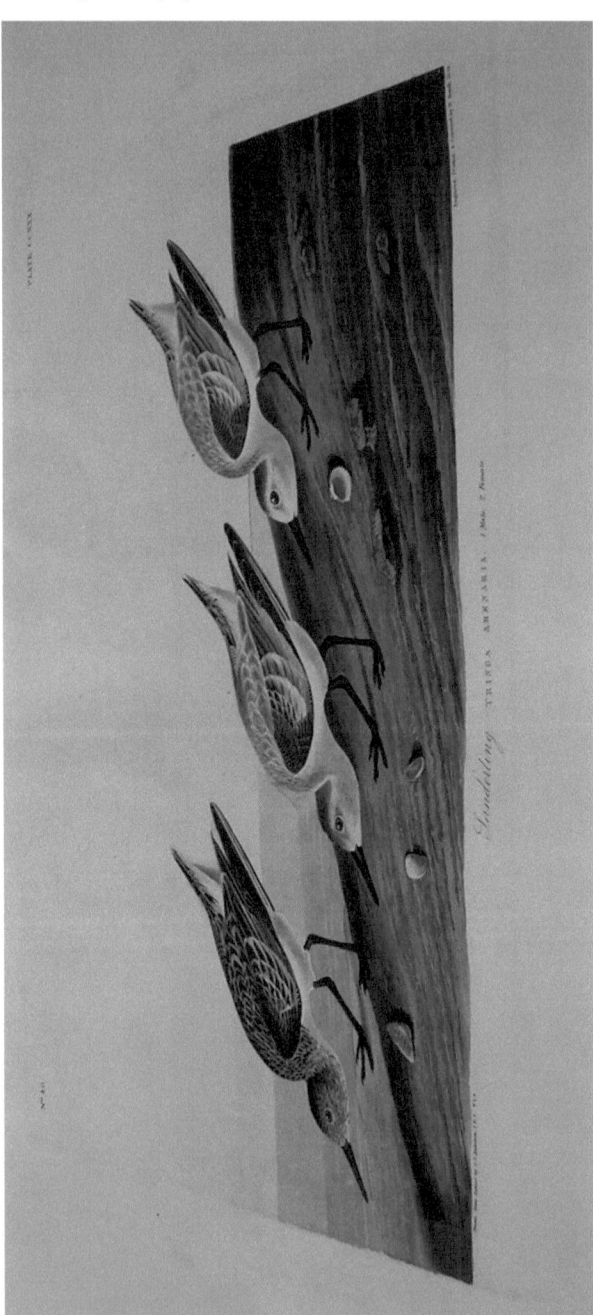

42. - Composite plate CCXXX

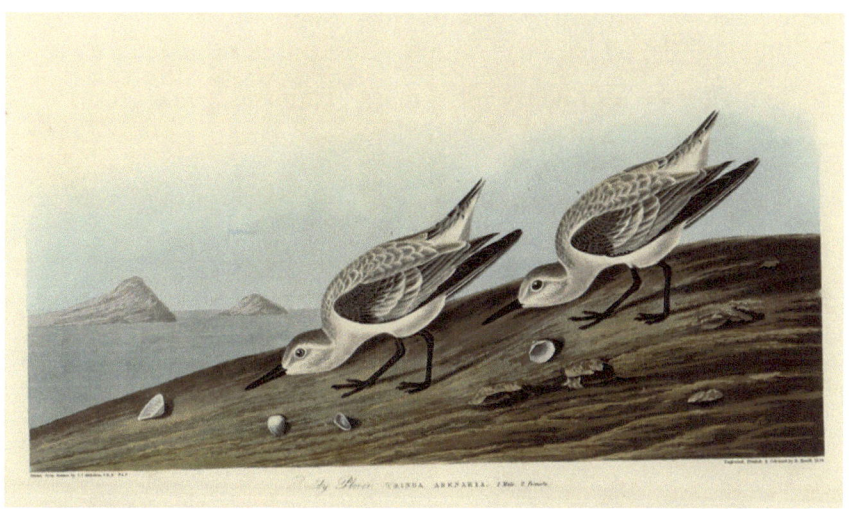

43. - Primary plate

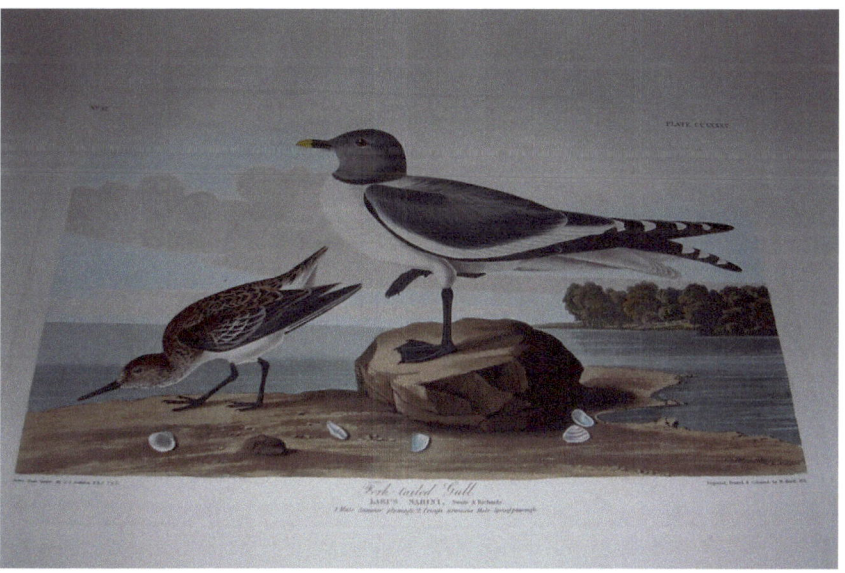

44. - Secondary plate

In the primary print, mountains or islands on the horizon are depicted in the background. These features were eliminated due to the positioning of the added bird. Ground coloring is extended on the left, to the edge of the secondary plate mark. This additional coloring appears to be of a slightly different shade.

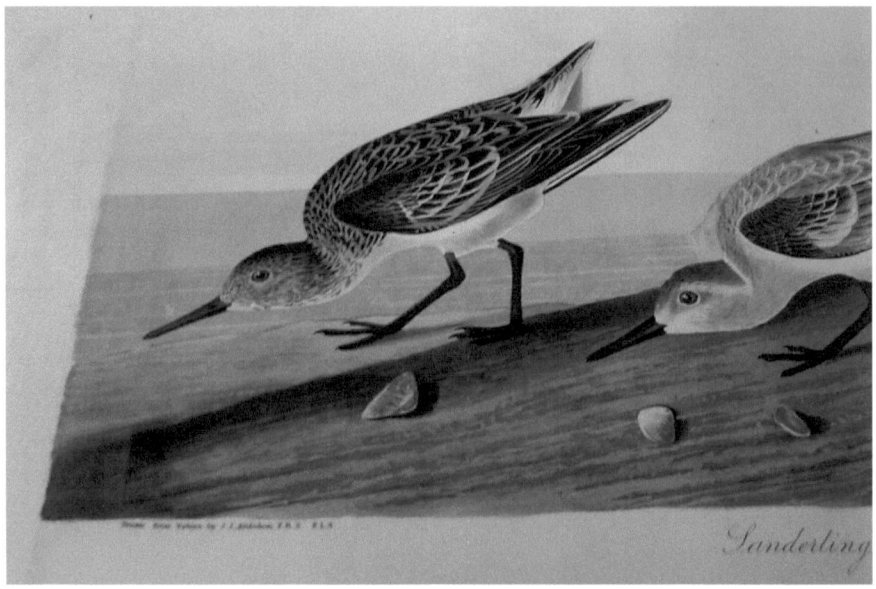

45. - Detail of composite plate

Both the primary and secondary plates show scattered sea shells on the ground below the figured birds. The authors, in addition to studing the Sanderling composite print in the Stark Museum collection, were also privileged to briefly examine the same plate in the collection of the John James Audubon Center at Mill Grove. In both of these prints, a shadow of sea shell could be observed. In the Mill Grove print, this "ghost" shell overlaps slightly the clearly visible shell.

In contrast, the "ghost" shell in the Stark Museum print is positioned to the left and does not overlap the visible shell at all.

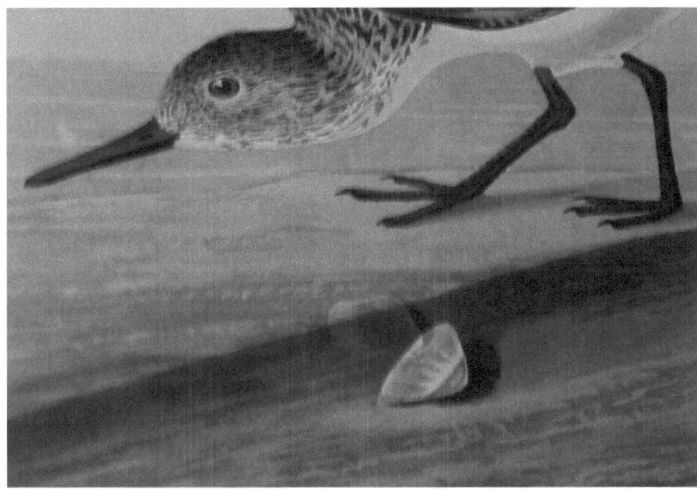

46. - Detail of composite plate from the set at Mill Grove. Note the distinct "ghost shell" and the relationship of the Sanderling's rear foot to the dark beach line.

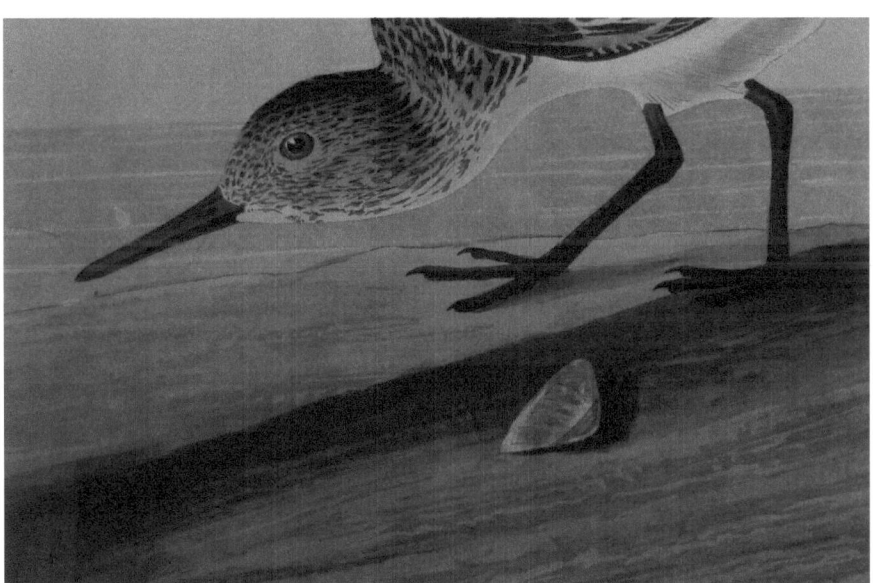

47. - Detail of composite plate from the set at the Stark Museum. Note the barely visible "ghost shell" and the relationship of the Sanderling's rear foot to the dark beach line.

The plate marks from the secondary plate are located 1 ½" to the left and 1/2" above the primary. (Note: Horizontally, the secondary plate mark was found not to be perfectly parallel to the primary, angling to about a ¼" at the upper left side.)

Louisiana Tanager (Plate CCCLIV)

This composite, picturing the present day Western Tanager, has the added image of a female from Plate CCCC which is positioned on the left side, center.

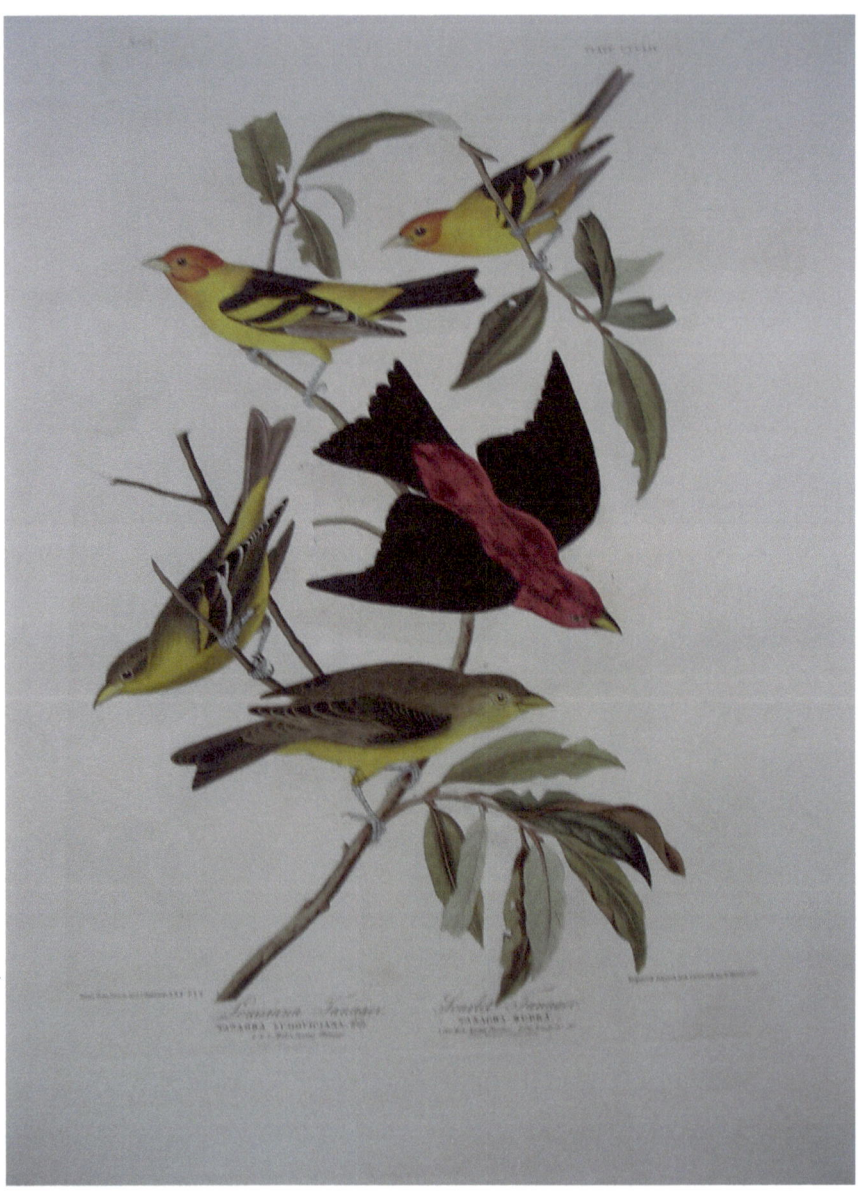

48. - Composite plate CCCLIV

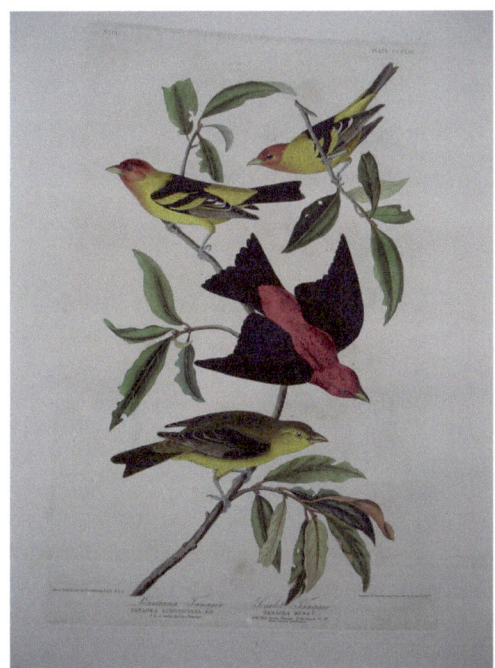

49. - Primary plate

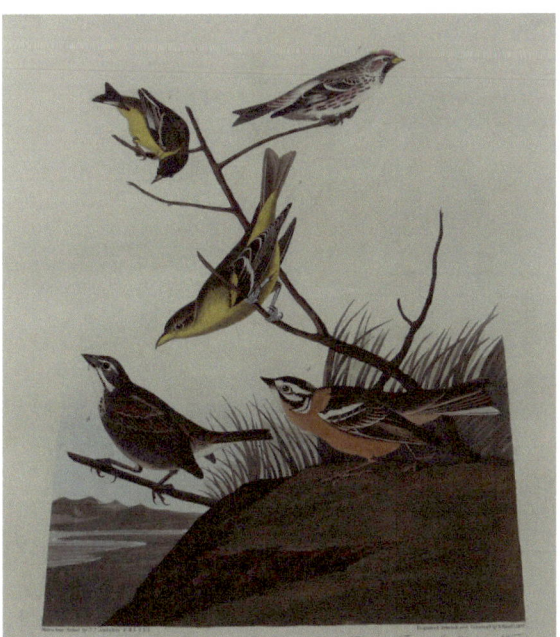

50. - Secondary plate

The leaves located directly to the left of the Scarlet Tanager in the primary plate have been removed in order to accommodate the added bird. The added bird is perched on a branch that has been extended out from behind the bottommost bird in this print.

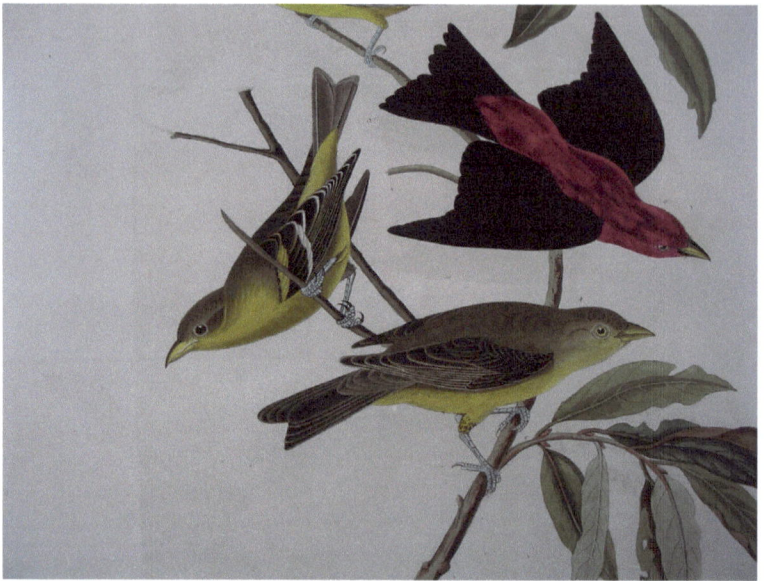

51. - Detail of composite plate

The Stark Museum copy of this composite print bears a handwritten notation below the printed Louisiana Tanager attribution: "3b Female".

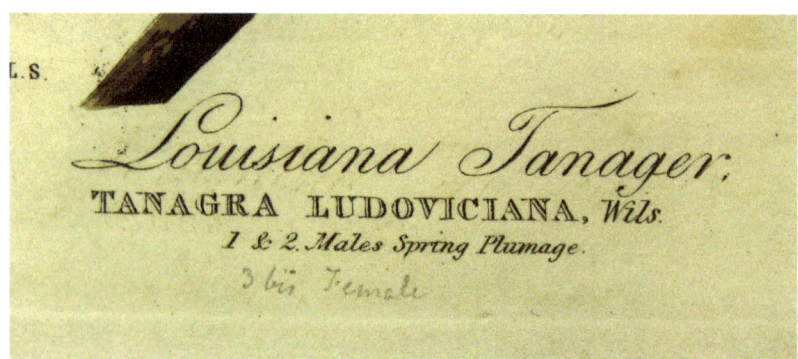

52. - Detail of composite plate

The plate marks of the secondary plate are positioned 2 1/8" down and 2 ½" to the left of the primary plate marks.

Mountain Mocking Bird and Varied Thrush
(Plate CCCLXIX)

This mixed species plate of the Varied Thrush and what we now know as the Sage Thrasher had added to it a female Varied Thrush from Plate CCCCXXXIII. The added bird has been placed in the lower right quadrant of the print. The new addition in this print is found standing on a branch that came from the secondary plate and has been melded to the branch that was cut off in the primary plate.

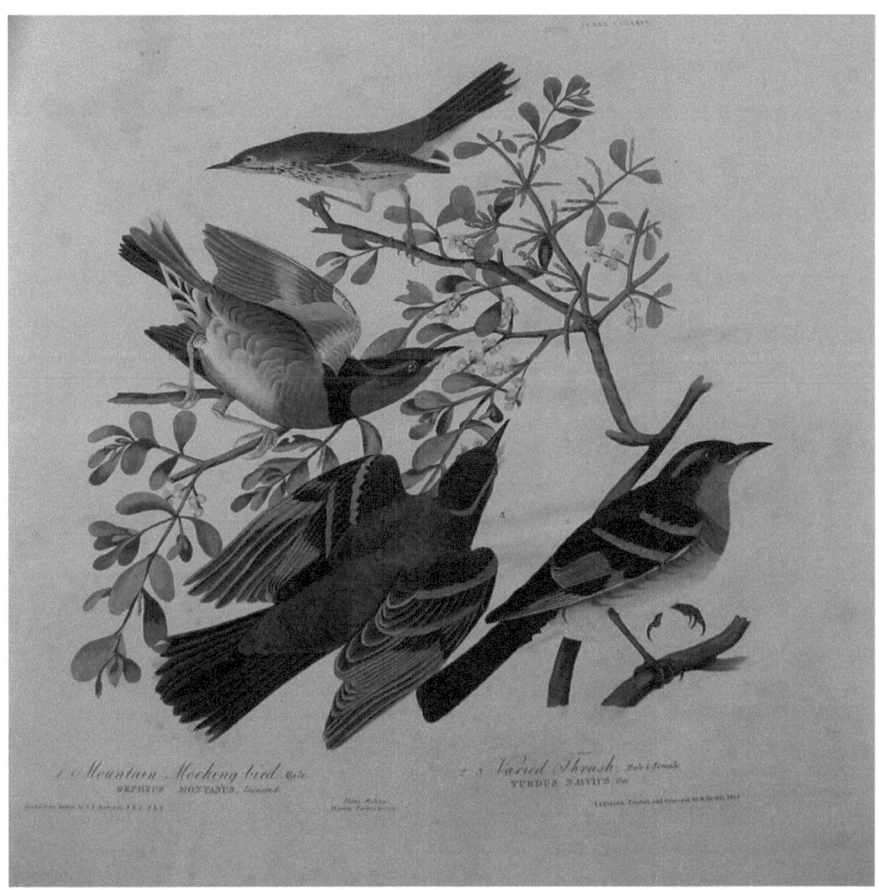

53. - Composite plate CCCLXIX

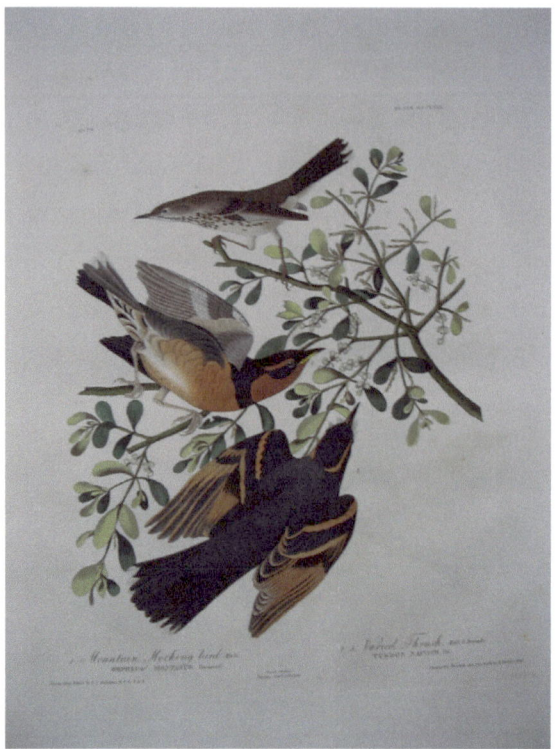

54. - Primary plate

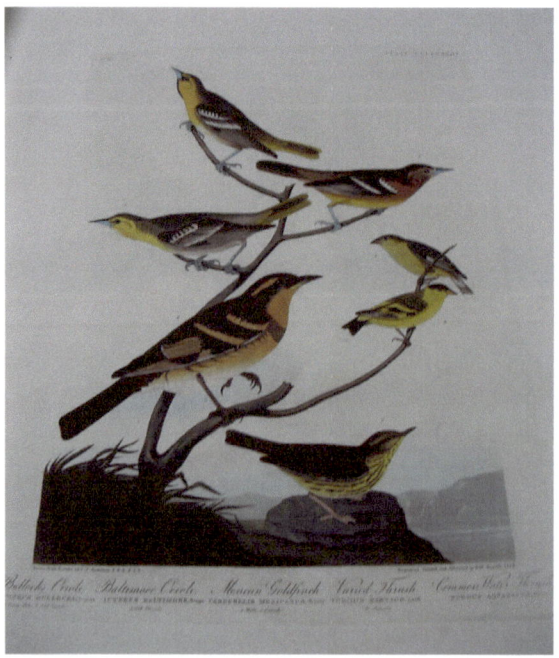

55. - Secondary plate

Close inspection reveals shadows of un-inked foliage and por-
tions of the Baltimore Oriole depicted on Plate CCCCXXXIII. Addi-
tionally, when viewed under a strong raking light, traces of the plate
legend from the secondary plate can be visualized.

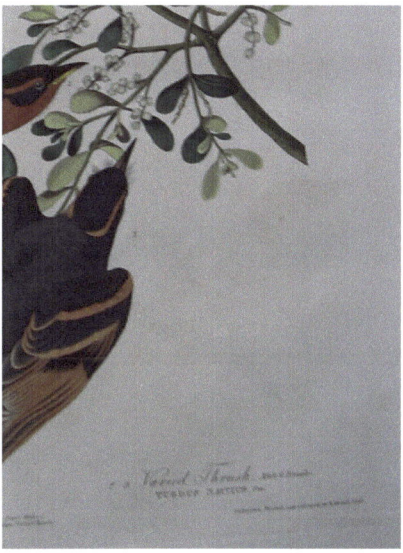

56. - Detail of primary plate

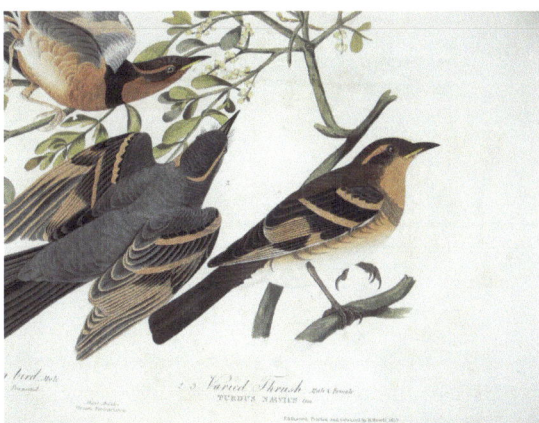

57. - Detail of composite plate

The secondary plate marks are located 2 5/8" lower and 6 15/16"
to the right of the primary plate marks. The horizontal plate marks created by the secondary copper plate extend fully to the right edge of the
paper. The added bird is positioned that it extends well past the right
side primary plate marks.

Evening Grosbeak and Spotted Grosbeak
(Plate CCCLXXIII)

Added to the three Black-headed Grosbeaks and the single Evening Grosbeak in this mixed species print is a female and young male Evening Grosbeak from Plate CCCCXXIV.

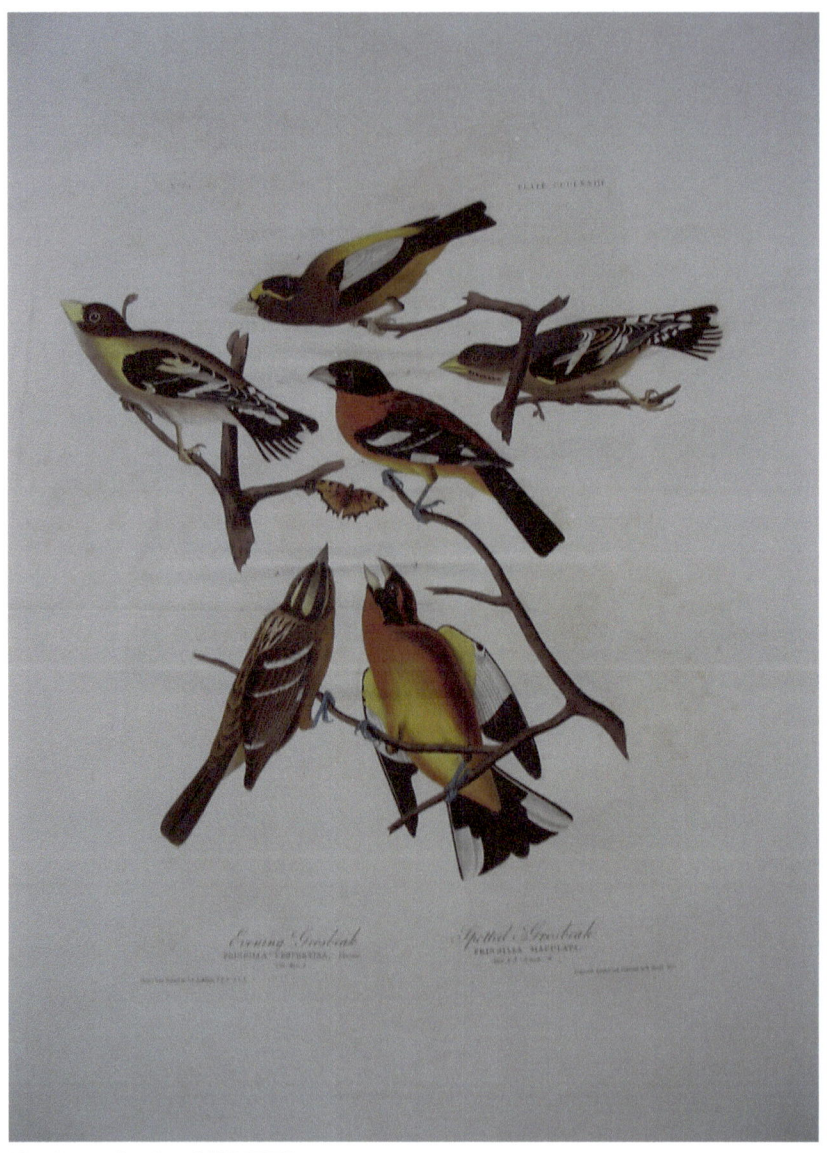

58. - Composite plate CCCLXXIII

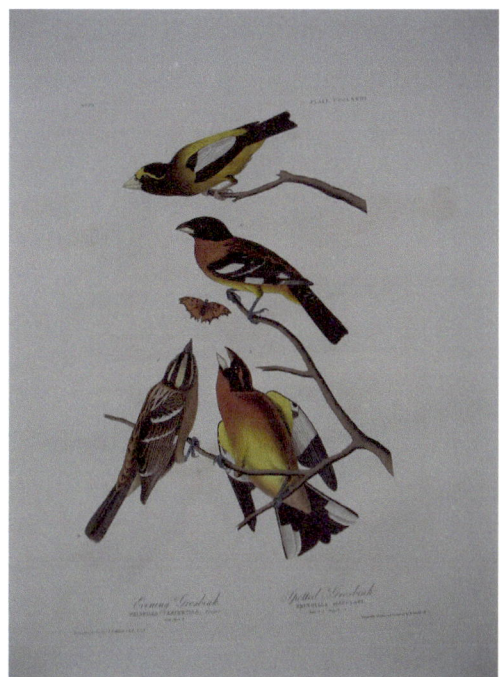

59. - Primary plate

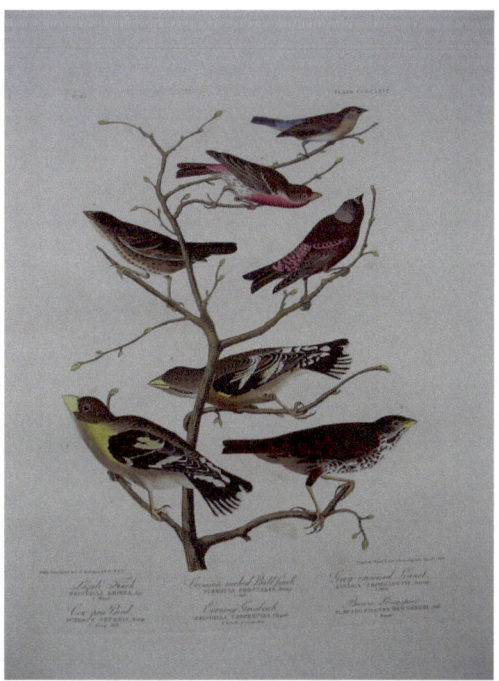

60. - Secondary plate

On the secondary plate from which the added birds are taken, the two birds are positioned vertically, one above the other.

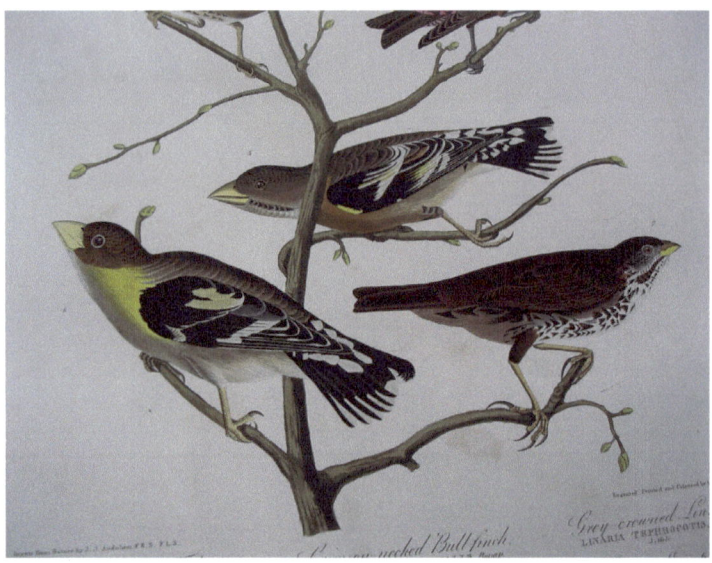

61. - Detail of secondary plate

On the composite print, the two added birds are positioned in the upper right and left quadrants. The young male positioned in the upper right of the composite is sitting on the central branch depicted in the secondary plate, which in turn has been blended into a branch from the primary plate.

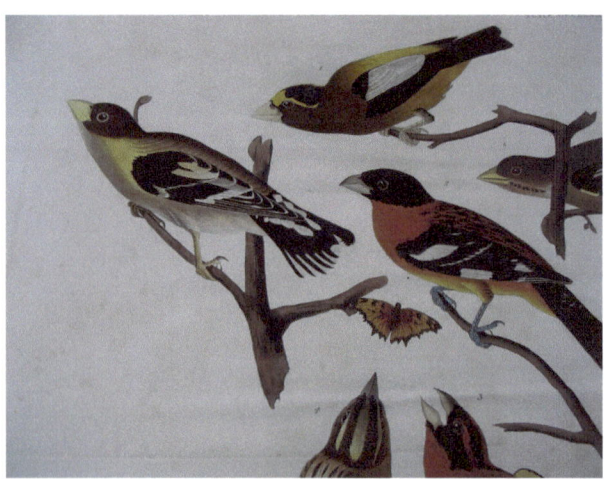

62. - Detail of upper left quadrant of composite plate

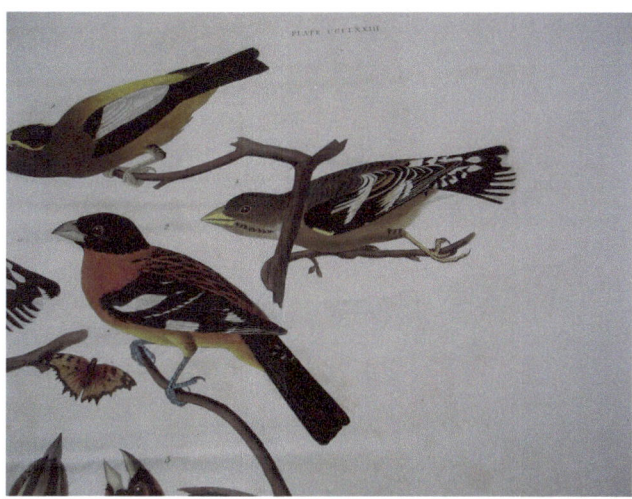

63. - Detail of upper right quadrant of composite plate

Because the two added birds were split apart, this composite print had to undergo the printing process three times, resulting in three sets of plate marks. The first set of secondary plate marks are positioned 4 5/8" to the right and 6" up from the primary plate mark. The second set of plate marks is located 2 7/8" to the left and 8 ¼" up from the primary plate marks. Likely because of the stress of three pressings, this composite plate shows a marked ripple or wave in the paper.

Bullock's Oriole, Yellow-headed Troopial and Nuttall's Starling (Plate CCCLXXXVIII)

The later two species in this mixed print are presently know as Yellow-headed Blackbird and Tricolored Blackbird respectively. A male and female Bullock's Oriole were added from Plate CCCCXXXIII to create this composite plate. The immature male is positioned in the upper left quadrant and the female is located in the lower left. The branch upon which the Nuttall's Starling is standing in the primary print has been cut off. However, in the composite, this branch extends to the lower left of the plate with the added birds perched on offshoots of this branch.

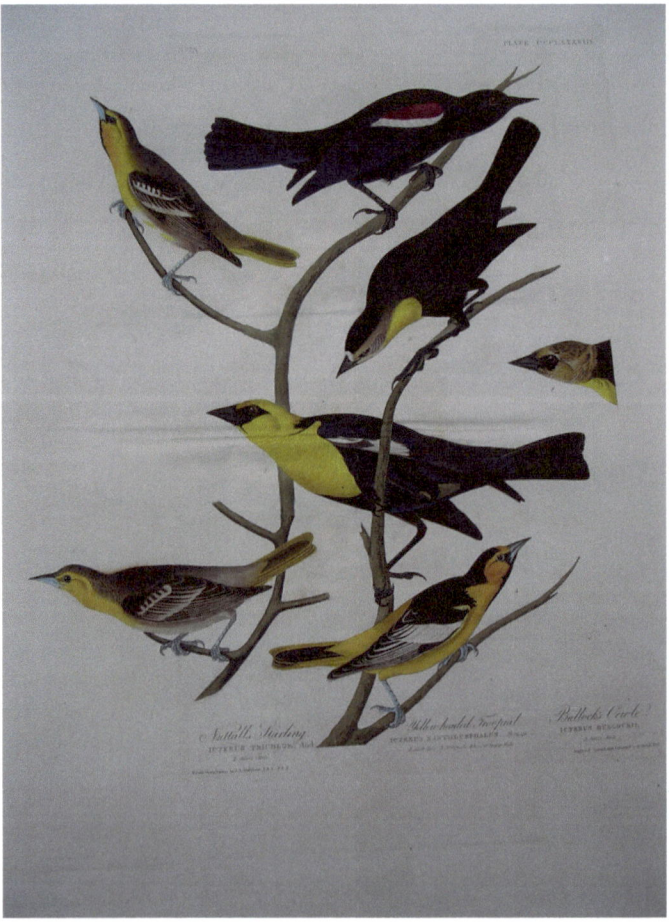

64. - Composite plate CCCLXXXVIII

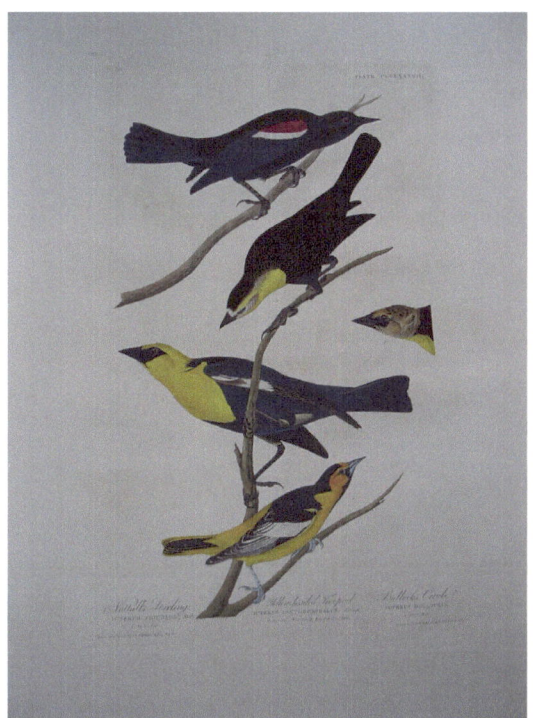

65. - Primary plate

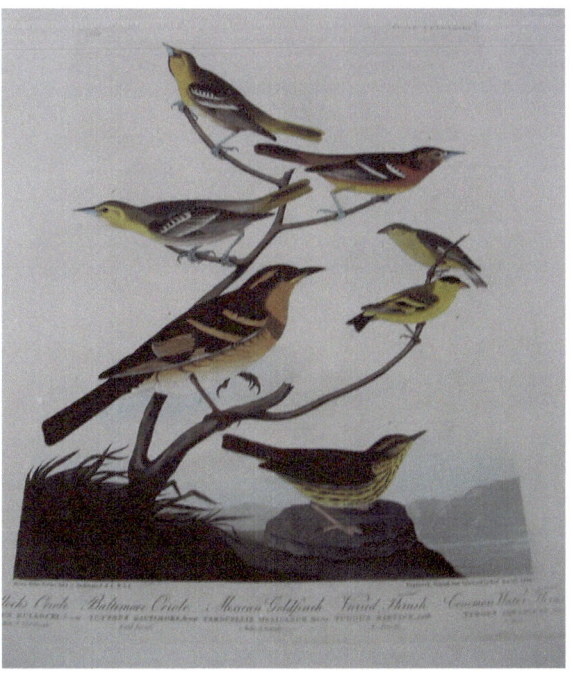

66. - Secondary plate

As in the previous composite plate, this print displays a stress ripple in the paper.

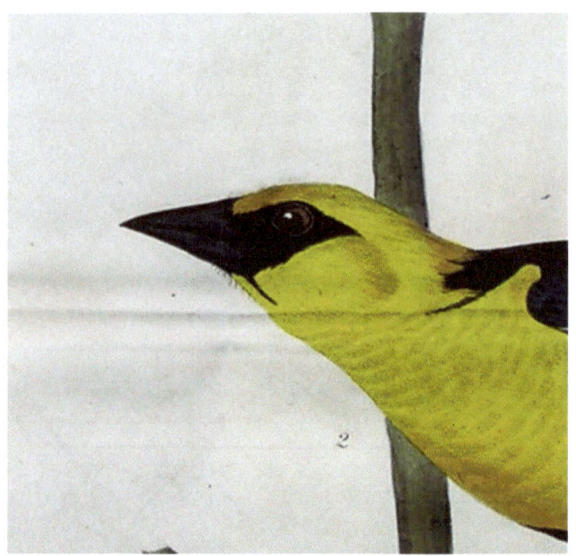

67. - Detail of composite plate showing stress ripple in paper

Also as in the previously described composite plate, this plate as well bears three sets of plate marks. The first set of secondary plate marks is positioned 3 3/8" to the left and 1 3/4" down from the primary plate mark. The second set if located 3" to the left and 7 1/4" down from the primary plate mark.

Lazuli Finch, Clay-coloured Finch and Oregon Snow Finch (Plate CCCXCVIII)

These three species are now named Lazuli Bunting, Clay-colored Sparrow and Dark-eyed Junco. The composite was made by the addition of a female Lazuli Bunting from Plate CCCCXXIV which is positioned in the upper right quadrant of the print.

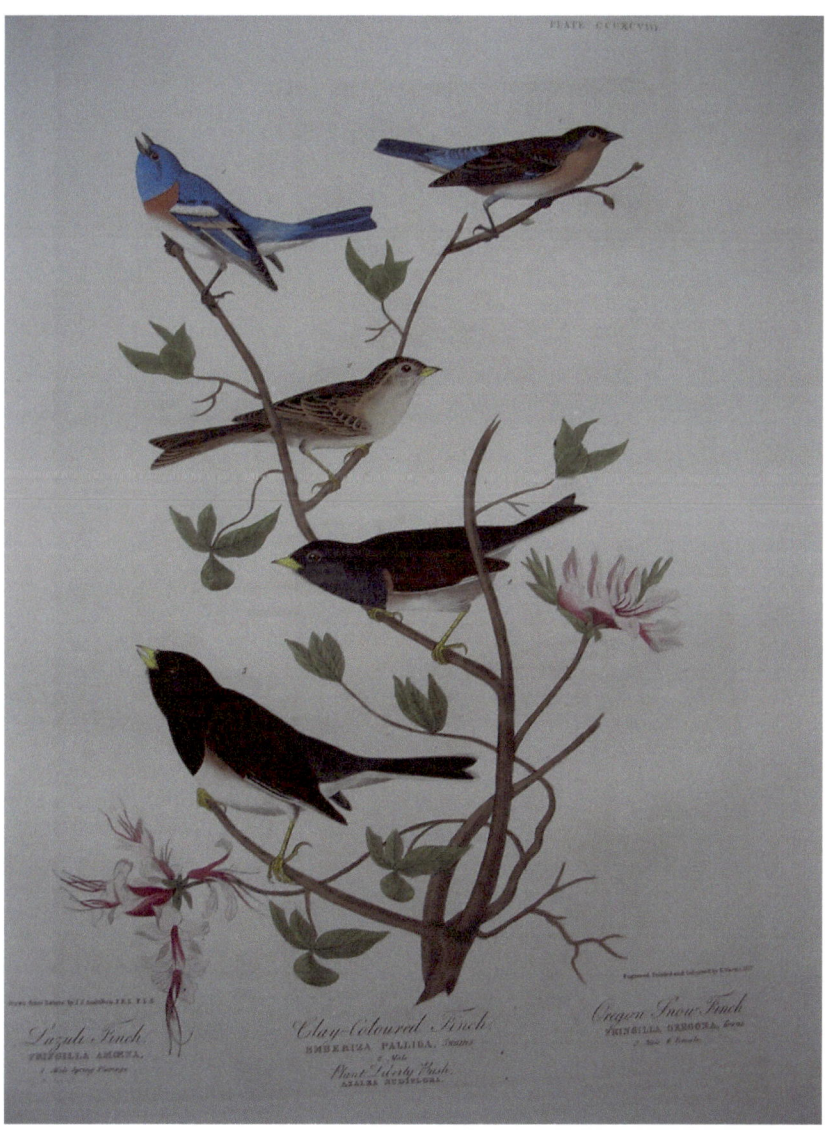

68. - Composite plate CCCXCVIII

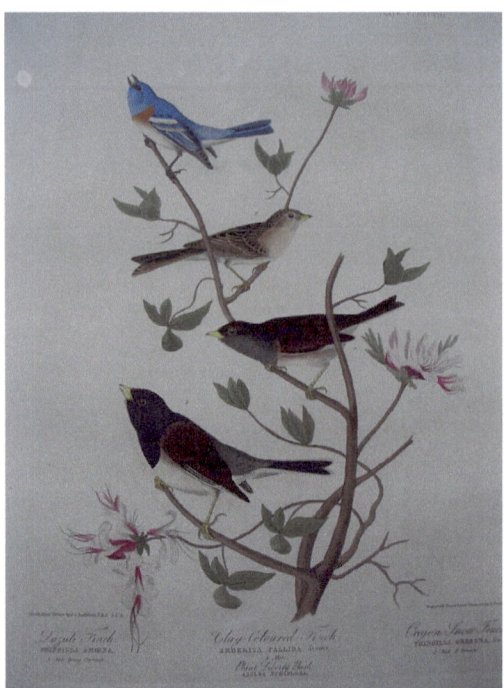

69. - Primary plate

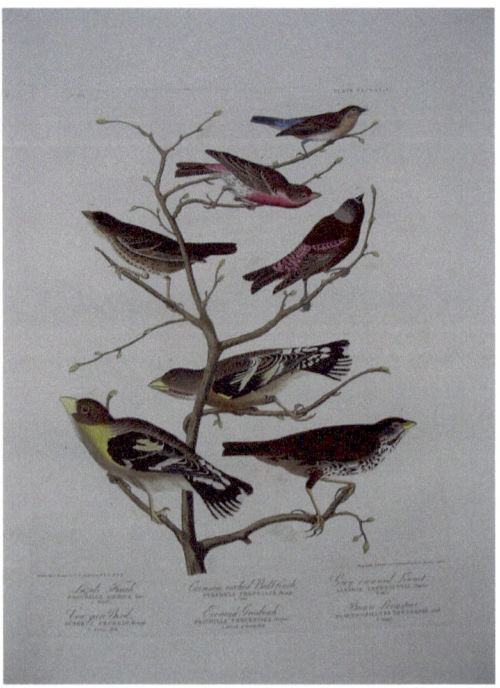

70. - Secondary plate

To add the female Lazuli Bunting, Havell removed the topmost azalea flower and extended a branch upon which the added bird is perched.

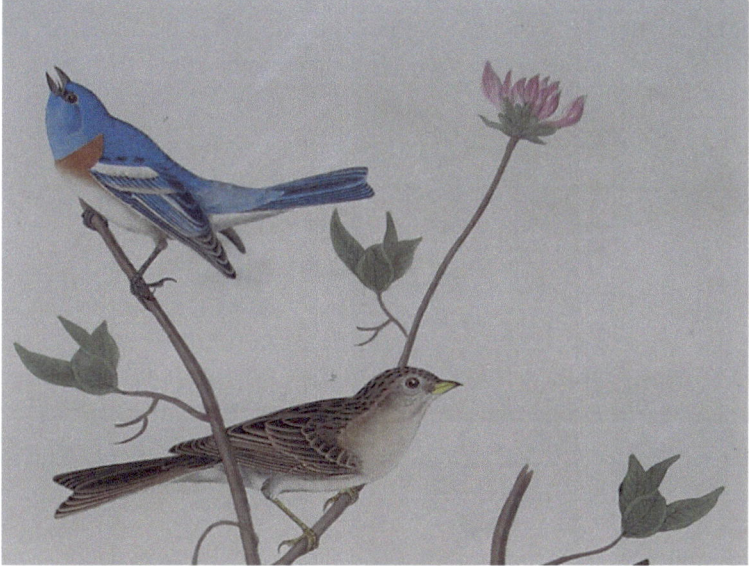

71. - Detail of primary plate

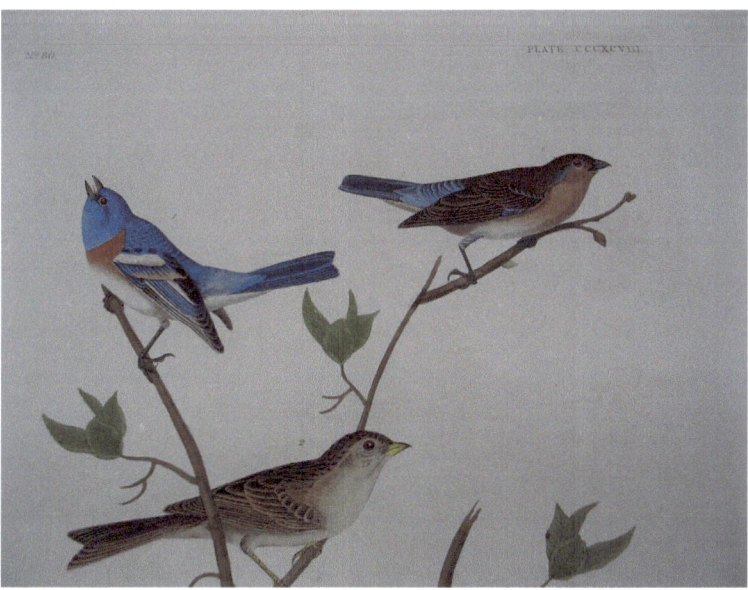

72. - Detail of composite plate

Under a strong raking light, the plate number from the secondary plate could be observed. In the lower attributions, below the engraved legend for Lazuli Finch was found a handwritten penciled notation: "2. Female".

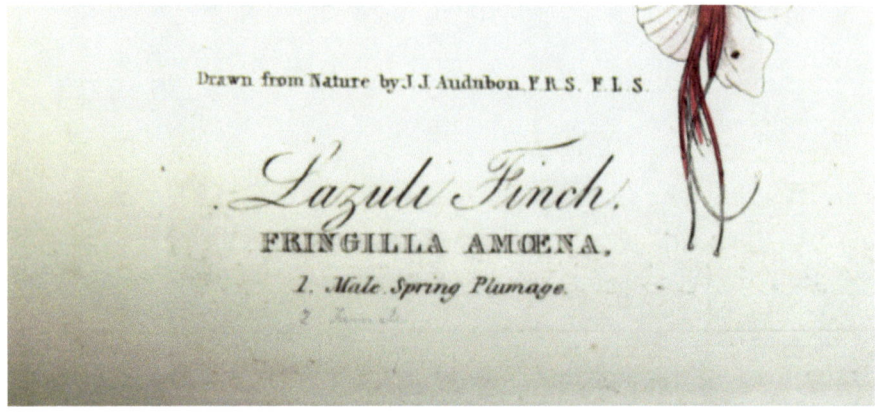

73. - Detail of composite plate

Both on the front, and more so on the reverse, where the added image is positioned, is a visible 5" X 7" rectangle suggesting that Havell may have used some type of material to mask off a part of the secondary copper plate during the printing process.

Primary, Secondary, and Composite Plates

Audubon anticipated that upon the completion of *Birds of America*, a subscriber would have his plates bound into four volumes, the first three containing 100 plates each and the last containing the remaining 135. While a few editions deviated from this format, most surviving editions follow this protocol. The table below sets forth in which volume a researcher is likely to locate the primary, secondary and composite plates.

Composite Plate and Primary Plate

Volume 1
>Plate XII (12) – Baltimore Oriole
>Plate XXIII (23) – Maryland Yellow Throat

Volume 2
>Plate CVII (107) – Canada Jay
>Plate CX (110) – Hooded Warbler
>Plate CXXXV (135) – Blackburnian Warbler
>Plate CXL (140) – Pine Creeping Warbler

Volume 3
>Plate CCIX (209) – Wilson's Plover
>Plate CCXXX (230) – Sanderling

Volume 4
>Plate CCCLIV (354) – Louisiana Tanager
>Plate CCCLXIX (369) – Mountain Mocking Bird & Varied Thrush
>Plate CCCLXXIII (373) – Evening Grosbeak & Spotted Grosbeak
>Plate CCCLXXXVIII (388) – Bullock's Oriole, Yellow-headed Troopial & Nuttall's Starling

Plate CCCXCVIII (398) – Lazuli Finch, Clay-coloured Finch & Oregon Snow Finch

Secondary Plates

Volume 1

Plate IX (9) – Selby's Flycatcher (Added to Plate CX)

Plate XXIV (24) – Roscoe's Yellow Throat (Added to Plate XXIII)

Plate XXX (30) – Vigor's Vireo (Added to Plate CXL)

Volume 2

None

Volume 3

Plate CCLXXXIV (284) – Wilson's Plover (Added to Plate CCIX)

Plate CCLXXXV (285) Sanderling (Added to Plate CCXXX)

Volume 4

Plate CCCXCIX (399) – Blackburnian Warbler (Added to Plate CXXXV)

Plate CCCC (400) – Louisiana Tanager (Added to Plate CCCLIV)

Plate CCCCXIX (419) – Canada Jay (Added to Plate CVII)

Plate CCCCXXIV (424) – Lazuli Finch AND Evening Grosbeak

[NOTE: One image of the Lazuli Finch was added to Plate CCCXCVIII and two images of the Evening Grosbeak were added to Plate CCCLXXIII]

Plate CCCCXXXIII (433) – Bullock's Oriole AND Baltimore Oriole AND Varied Thrush

[NOTE: Two images of Bullock's Oriole were added to Plate CCCLXXXVIII; one image of Baltimore Oriole added to Plate XII and one image of Varied Thrush was added to Plate CCCLXIX]

Appendix I
The Order of the Stark Musuem Set of Birds of America

Noted Audubon scholars such as Susanne Low, Gregory Nobles and Waldemar Fries have all written that the three completed sets of *The Birds of America* which contain the additional 13 composite plates were all bound, at the request of Audubon, Phillips and Harris, in systematic order. "Indeed, although Audubon did bind his own copies of the plates into four volumes[14], he nonetheless rearranged the order of the plates in his own personal copy, as did two of his close friends, Edward Harris and Dr. Benjamin Phillips. In these three copies of *The Birds of America*, the plates do not follow the standard order in which Audubon produced them; rather, they have been bound in accordance with the ornithological classification scheme that Audubon later developed in *A Synopsis of the Birds of America* (1839). Thus, in Audubon's own copy of *The Birds of America* (which is now in the H.J. Lutcher Stark Museum in Orange, Texas), the first volume begins not with the famous image of the 'Great American Cock, or Wild Turkey,' which was the original Plate I, but with the 'Turkey Vulture' (Plate 426), which came toward the very end of the standard order in *The Birds of America*." (Nobles, 2005)

In Fries's discussion on the provenance of the Stark Museum's set, he noted that "the plates were numbered according to the order in which they were bound." (Fries, 1973) In our examination of the Stark set, the authors confirmed that the composites are bound as follows:
Volume 1
    43 – Hooded Warbler

---

[14] While most copies were bound into four volumes, Audubon had his personal copy bound into five. In a letter dated November 5, 1861, authored by Audubon's son, John Woodhouse Audubon, wherein he is offering to sell his father's copy of *Birds of America*, he offers this description: "The Birds of America by J.J. Audubon bound in 5 vols. by Herring of London." (J.W. Audubon, 1861, *in litt.*)

56 – Pine Creeping Warbler

65 – Blackburnian Warbler

79 – Maryland Yellow Throat

Volume 2

133 – Lazuli Finch, Clay-coloured Finch & Oregon Snow Finch

165 – Evening Grosbeak & Spotted Grosbeak

168 – Louisiana Tanager

172 – Bullock's Oriole, Yellow-headed Troopial & Nuttall's Starling

176 – Baltimore Oriole

Volume 3

193 – Mountain Mocking Bird & Varied Thrush

215 – Canada Jay

Volume 4

287 – Wilson's Plover

306 – Sanderling

Volume 5

None

If the Stark set was bound in accordance with *A Synopsis of the Birds of America*, then presumably, the sequential listing and number assigned to each species described in the *Synopsis* should correspond with the above. Below is the number and sequence of where each of the 13 species which comprise the composite plates is described in *A Synopsis of the Birds of America*.

71 – Hooded Warbler

82 – Pine Creeping Wood-Warbler

87 – Blackburnian Warbler

102 – Maryland Yellow-throat

143 – Varied Thrush

171 – Lazuli Finch

207 – Evening Grosbeak

210 – Louisiana Tanager

217 – Baltimore Hangnest (Oriole)

218 – Bullock's Hangnest (Oriole)

234 – Canada Jay

320 – Wilson's Plover

339 – Sanderling Sandpiper

A cursory comparison of the two lists above shows that something is amiss. First, none of the numbers assigned to the Stark set match those in the *Synopsis*. Second, Varied Thrush in the Stark set is located before Canada Jay, yet in the *Synopsis*, it is described between Maryland Yellow Throat and Lazuli Finch. In like fashion, the Baltimore Oriole and Bullock's Oriole are bound in the Stark set in reverse order from where they occur in the *Synopsis*. (In addition, while the Baltimore Oriole and Bullock's Oriole appear consecutively in the *Synopsis*, they are separated by three other prints in the Stark set.)

While it is beyond the scope of this article and the resources of the authors to perform a detailed page by page comparison of each print ing the Stark set with *A Synopsis of the Birds of America*, the following may provide a starting point for future research. First, Audubon states in the preface to *A Synopsis of the Birds of America* that "This Synopsis, then, will afford a methodical catalogue of all the species hitherto discovered in the vast regions, extending from the northern confines of Mexico to the Polar Seas, and which have been described, with few exceptions, depicted in the works above named." (Audubon, 1839) The "works above named" are *The Birds of America* and *Ornithological Biography, or an Account of the Habits of the Birds of the United States*. Low writes in *A Guide to Audubon's Birds of America* that the total number of species depicted and described by Audubon between the above two works add up to 474. (449 species are depicted in *The Birds of America* plus an additional 25 described, but never painted, in *Ornithological Biography*.) Since, there are 491 species described in the *Synopsis*, then there must be 17 additional species which must constitute the "few exceptions" that Audubon neither depicted nor described previously. Could these 17 plus the 25 unpainted species from *Ornithological Biography* (plus those large birds such as Wild Turkey that had by necessity been depicted on multiple plates) explain why the numbers from the Stark set don't match those in the *Synopsis*? Perhaps, but even if they do, how does one explain that the Varied Thrush[15], Baltimore Oriole and Bullock's Oriole are bound utterly out of sequence?

If nothing else, the commonly held belief that the completed sets of Audubon, Harris and Phillips were bound in the taxonomic order described in *A Synopsis of the Birds of America* requires a thorough re-examination.

---

[15] The Varied Thrush primary plate also depicts the Mountain Mocking bird. In this plate, the Varied Thrush is listed as the second species portrayed. The Mountain Mocking bird in the *Synopsis* is listed as the 139th bird described, four positions before the Varied Thrush. Hence, even if the Mountain Mocking bird was the species used to determine the sequence of binding in the Stark set, this plate is still bound out of sequence.

Literature Cited

Audubon, J. J. 1831-1839. Ornithological Biography, or an Account of the Habits of the Birds of the United State of America; Accompanied by Descriptions of the Objects Represented in the Work Entitled The Birds of America, and Interspersed with Delineations of American Scenery and Manners. 5 Vols. A. Black, Edinburgh.

Audubon, J.J. 1839. A Synopsis of the Birds of North America. A. Black, Edinburgh.

Fries, W.H. 1973. The Double Elephant Folio. The Story of Audubon's *Birds of America.* Zenaida Publishing, Inc., Amherst, Massachusetts.

Goddu, J. The Making of Audubon's The Birds of America. The Magazine Antiques, Nov. 2002: 112-121.

Low, S.M. 2002. A Guide to Audubon's *Birds of America.* William Reese Company & Donald A. Heald, New Haven and New York.

Nobles, G.H. 2005. Ornithology and Enterprise: Making and Marketing John James Audubon's *The Birds of America.* American Antiquarian Society, Worcester, Massachusetts.

Steiner, B. 2003. Audubon Art Prints: A Collector's Guide to Every Edition, University of South Carolina Press, Columbia, SC.

Wilson, A. 1808-1814. American Ornithology; or, The Natural History of the Birds of the United States: Illustrated with Plates Engraved and colored from Original Drawings taken from Nature. 9 Vols. Bradford and Inskeep, Philadelphia.

Manuscripts Cited

Letter from John Woodhouse Audubon to J.T. Johnston; November 5, 1861. Audubon Archives, 11.2.105.B. Courtesy of the Stark Museum of Art, Orange, TX.

Letter from Victor Gifford Audubon (with addendum by John James Audubon) to Robert Havell; August 20, 1938. John James Audubon papers, call number MS Am 1482 (243). By permission of the Houghton Library, Harvard University.

Letter from Victor Gifford Audubon to Robert Havell; August 26, 1938. John James Audubon papers, call number MS Am 1482 (244). By permission of the Houghton Library, Harvard University.

Letter from Victor Gifford Audubon to Robert Havell; September 26, 1938. John James Audubon papers, call number MS Am 1482 (245). By permission of the Houghton Library, Harvard University.

Additional Sources

Audubon, J.J. 1838. The Birds of America, Volume I
engraving and aquatint on paper, hand-colored, bound
38 1/4 x 25 1/2 (97.2 x 64.8 cm)
SMA #11.1.2.A

Audubon, J.J. 1838. The Birds of America, Volume II
engraving and aquatint on paper, hand-colored, bound
38 1/4 x 25 1/2 (97.2 x 64.8 cm)
SMA #11.1.2.B

Audubon, J.J. 1838. The Birds of America, Volume III
engraving and aquatint on paper, hand-colored, bound
38 1/4 x 25 1/2 (97.2 x 64.8 cm)
SMA #11.1.2.C

Audubon, J.J. 1838. The Birds of America, Volume IV
engraving and aquatint on paper, hand-colored, bound
38 1/4 x 25 1/2 (97.2 x 64.8 cm)
SMA #11.1.2.D

Audubon, J.J. 1838. The Birds of America, Volume V
engraving and aquatint on paper, hand-colored, bound
38 1/4 x 25 1/2 (97.2 x 64.8 cm)
SMA #11.1.2.E

Audubon, J. J. and Irmscher, C. 1999 John James Audubon: Writings
and Drawings. The Library of America, New York.

Audubon, J.J. and Rhodes, R. 2006. John James Audubon: The
Audubon Reader. Alfred A. Knopf, New York.

Blaugrund, A. and Stebbins, T.E. 1993. John James Audubon: The
Watercolors for *The Birds of America*. Villard Books, Random
House, New York.

Braun, R. 1996. Identifying Audubon Prints: Originals, States, Editions, Restrikes, and Facsimiles and Reproductions. Imprint, Vol. 21, No. 2: 12-22.

Brewer, T.M. 1880, Reminiscences of John James Audubon. Harper's New Monthly Magazine, Vol. 61, No. 365: 665-675.

Chalmers, J. 2003. Audubon in Edinburgh. NMS Publishing, Edinburgh.

Corning, H. 1930. Letters of John James Audubon, 1826-1840. 2 Vols. The Club of Odd Volumes, Boston.

Ford, A. 1987. The 1826 Journal of John James Audubon. Abbeville Press, New York.

Griswold, R.W. 1851. John James Audubon. The International Magazine of Literature, Art & Science, Vol. 2, No. 4: 469-474.

Hart-Davis, D. 2004. Audubon's Elephant: America's Greatest Naturalist and the Making of *The Birds of America*. Henry Holt and Co., New York.

Herrick, F.H. 1917. Audubon the Naturalist, A History of His Life and Times. 2 Vols. D. Appleton and Co., New York and London.

Rhodes, R. 2004. John James Audubon, The Making of an American. Alfred A. Knopf, New York.

Souder, W. 2004. Under a Wild Sky. North Point Press, New York.

Williams, G. A. 1916. Robert Havell, Junior, Engraver of Audubon's "Birds of America". The Print Collector's Quarterly, Vol. 6: 225-257

Acknowledgements

First and foremost, the authors would like to express their gratitude to the staff at the Stark Museum of Art in Orange, Texas for allowing us to examine, take measurements of and photograph each and every composite, primary and secondary plate. In particular, we are grateful for the help afforded by Jennifer Connors and Allison Evans who devoted an entire day out of their busy schedule to assist in this project. Furthermore, while we were performing our examinations of the various plates, Dr. Sarah Boehme took the time to locate some of the documentation that accompanied their acquisition of the Audubon volumes. These letters and manuscripts were invaluable, allowing us to fill in some gaps in our research.

In addition, thanks must be directed to the Houghton Library at Harvard University which provided us with copies of the letters from Victor Gifford Audubon to Havell that authorized the production of the composite plates.

An appreciation must be extended to Nancy Powell at the John James Audubon Center at Mill Grove. She graciously allowed us to examine one of the composite plates in their holdings. It was this initial foray that became the impetus for this project.

Our gratitude is extended to Eileen Mathias at The Academy of Natural Science in Philadelphia for arranging to have one of the few remaining copper plates brought out of storage for photographing.

Lastly, the authors extend their gratitude to Jane Henderson whose editorial assistance was invaluable.

Notes

www.ingramcontent.com/pod-product-compliance
Lightning Source LLC
Chambersburg PA
CBHW041102180526
45172CB00001B/71